I Can Cook

by

Mariette W. Hopman
and
Nirbhay N. Singh

Illustrations: Peter Fitzpatrick

Oxford University Press 1991

Oxford University Press
Walton Street
Oxford OX2 6DP

Oxford New York Toronto
Delhi Bombay Calcutta Madras Karachi
Petaling Jaya Singapore Hong Kong Tokyo
Nairobi Dar es Salaam Cape Town
Melbourne Auckland
and associated companies in
Berlin Ibadan

First published in New Zealand by Flour Power Press, 1986

First published in the United Kingdom by Oxford University Press, 1991

ISBN 0 19 8327862

Printed in Great Britain

Contents

Introduction

I Can Cook provides a bank of straightforward, photocopyable recipes for those teaching beginners in the kitchen. Teachers and carers may wish to begin with the simpler recipes so that the student can gain confidence in cooking by being able to achieve an easy goal. Many people may be able to use this book without additional assistance. For others, some assistance may initially be necessary, if only to establish the new cook's self-confidence in preparing a dish. However, it is wise to gradually withdraw such assistance as the person is increasingly able to manage by himself or herself. After all, the aim of *I Can Cook* is to establish self-reliance in cooking.

Happy cooking!

In the Kitchen

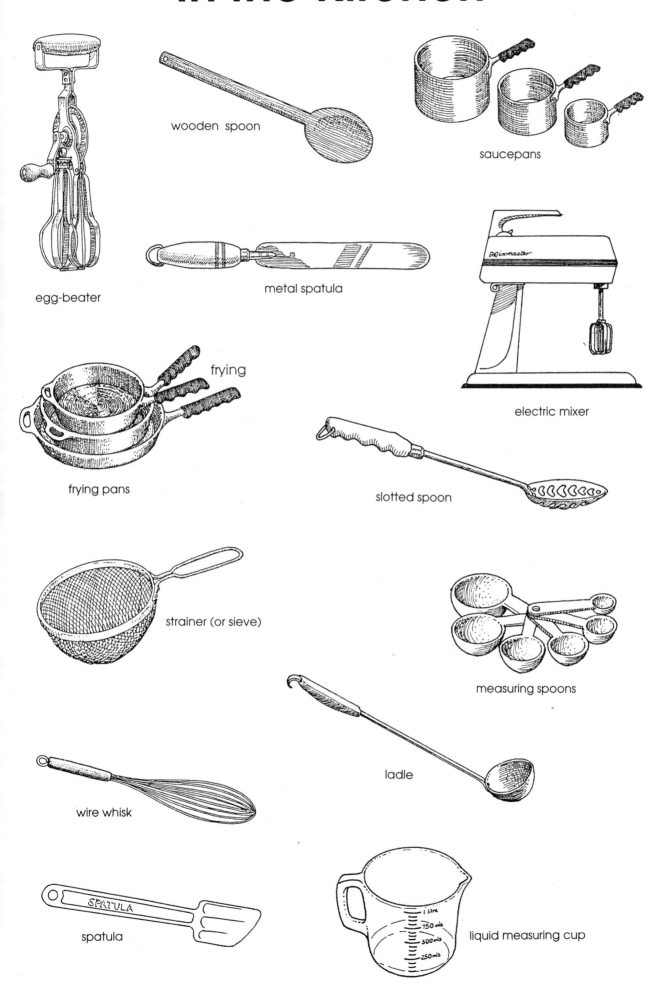

wooden spoon

saucepans

egg-beater

metal spatula

electric mixer

frying pans

slotted spoon

strainer (or sieve)

measuring spoons

wire whisk

ladle

spatula

liquid measuring cup

Utensils

Baking tray
Blender
Bowl
Chopping board
Colander
Cup
Dessert bowl
Egg beater
Electric mixer
Fork
Frying pan
Glasses
Grater
Kettle
Knives
Ladle
Large baking dish
Lemon squeezer
Liquid measuring cup
Metal spatula
Mixing bowl
Oven mitt

Pie dish
Plate
Potato masher
Potato peeler
Rolling pin
Rubber scraper
Saucepans
Saucer
Serving bowl
Slotted spoon
Soup bowl
Spatula
Spoons for measuring
Sieve
Tablespoon
Teaspoon
Tin opener
Toaster
Tongs
Wire rack
Wire whisk
Wooden spoon

Using the cooker

Oven temperatures

deg. C	deg. F	Gas Mark
40	275	1
150	300	2
160	325	3
180	350	4
190	375	5
200	400	6

Hints

<u>Tablespoonful and teaspoonful</u>   Do not use a heaped spoonful but instead just a rounded spoonful.

(a/w showing heaped and rounded spoonfuls)

<u>Boil (boiling)</u>   When the ring is on **HIGH** or **MEDIUM** and the water (or whatever is in the saucepan) is bubbling a lot.

<u>Simmer (simmering)</u>   When the ring is on **LOW** and the water (or whatever is in the saucepan) is bubbling very gently.

<u>Filling a saucepan</u>   Do not fill the saucepan more than half full of water when you are going to heat it on the ring.

<u>Sift</u> Putting flour (and sometimes baking powder/soda) into a sieve over a bowl and shaking the sieve gently so that no lumps go into the bowl.

<u>Salt and pepper</u>   You only ever need to add a pinch of salt and pepper to the savoury recipes.

You must make sure that the dishes you use in the oven and grill are 'oven proof'. This means that they will not break if they get hot.

Measures

You may notice that other cookery books use different measures to the spoonfuls and cupfuls used here. They measure in pounds and ounces (lbs and oz) or, more likely, kilograms and grams (kg and g). You need some kitchen scales if you are going to use these measures. The chart below gives a rough guide to the different measures although you should only use one set of measures at a time for each recipe.

Ounces	Grams (approximately)
1	25
2	50
3	75
4	100
5	150
6	175
7	200
8	225
9	250
10	275
11	300
12	350
13	375
14	400
15	425
16 (1lb)	450

Breakfast

Boiled Eggs

For 1 person

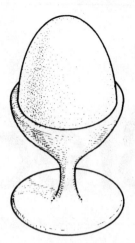

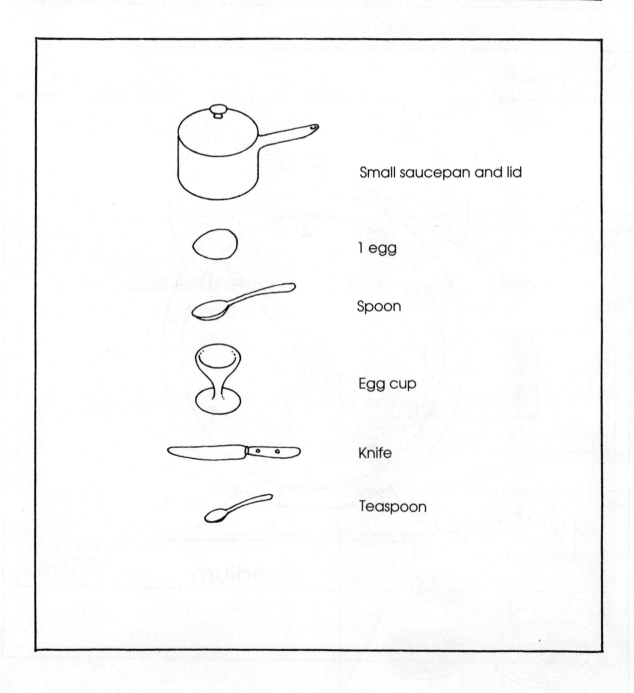

Small saucepan and lid

1 egg

Spoon

Egg cup

Knife

Teaspoon

1 **Wash your hands.**

Half-fill the saucepan with cold water.

2

Carefully place an egg into the water with the spoon.

3

Cover the saucepan with the lid.

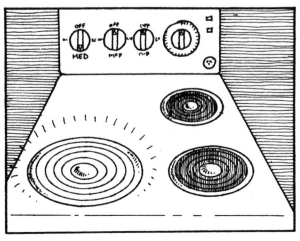

4

Turn the ring on to **medium**.

5

Place the saucepan on the ring so that the water can boil.

6

When the water has boiled, turn the ring **off**.

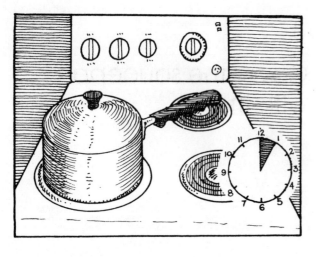

7

Let the egg stand in the water for 3 to 5 minutes.

8

Then add some cold water.

12

9

Lift the egg out with the spoon.

10

Place the egg into an egg cup.

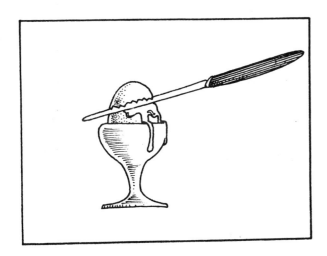

11

Cut open the egg with the knife.

12

Eat the egg with the spoon.

Fried Eggs

For 1 person

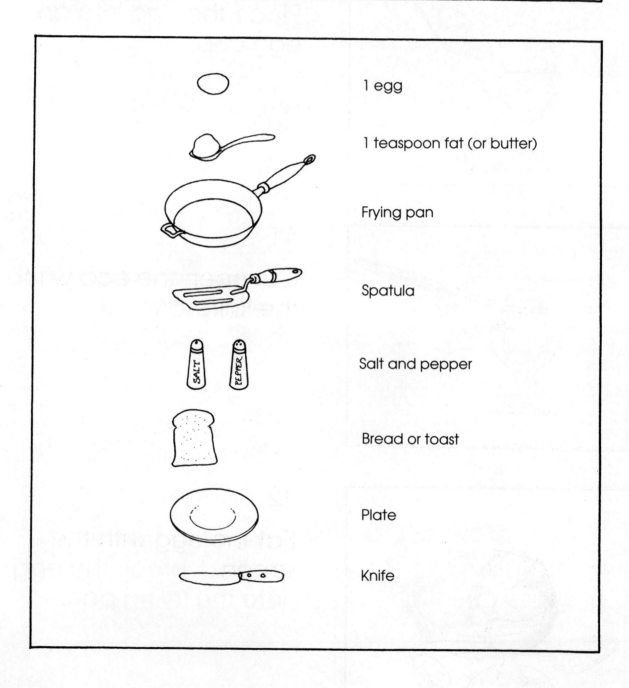

	1 egg
	1 teaspoon fat (or butter)
	Frying pan
	Spatula
	Salt and pepper
	Bread or toast
	Plate
	Knife

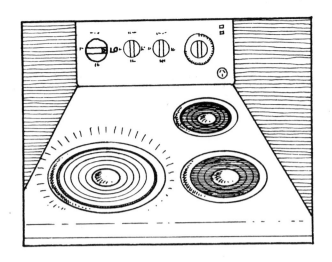

1 **Wash your hands.**

Turn the ring on to **low**.

2

Put 1 teaspoon of fat into the frying pan.

3

Put the frying pan on to the ring so the fat can melt.

4

When the fat has melted, break the egg into the frying pan.

5

Wait several minutes for the egg to cook.

6

Turn the egg on to the other side with the spatula.

7

Wait several minutes for the other side of the egg to cook.

8

Turn off the stove.

16

9

Put the egg on to a piece of toast or bread using the spatula.

10

Sprinkle a little salt and pepper on the egg.

Poached Eggs

For 1 person

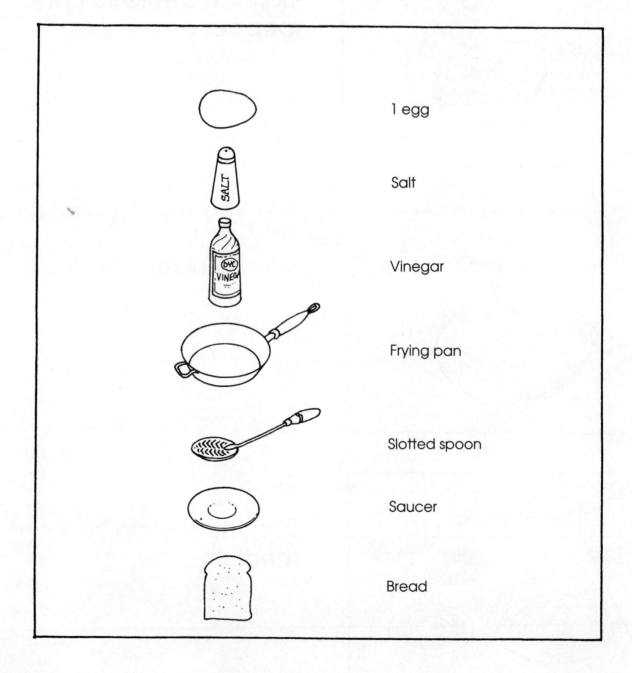

1 egg

Salt

Vinegar

Frying pan

Slotted spoon

Saucer

Bread

18

1 **Wash your hands.**

Fill the frying pan with water at least $2\frac{1}{2}$ centimetres (an inch) deep.

2

Sprinkle a little salt into the water.

3

Add a shake of vinegar.

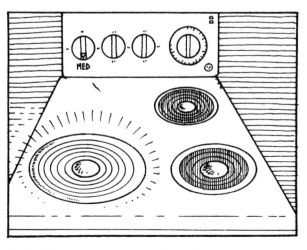

4

Turn the ring on to **medium**.

5

Put the frying pan on to the ring so the water can boil.

6

When the water has boiled, turn the ring **off**.

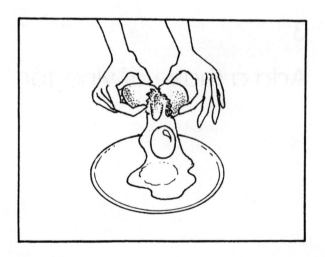

7

Break an egg into the saucer.

8

Slip the egg from the saucer into the water.

20

9

Put the lid on the frying pan.

10

Wait 3 to 5 minutes till the white of the egg is firm.

11

Lift the egg out with the slotted spoon.

12

Place the egg on a piece of toast or bread.

Scrambled Eggs

For 1 person

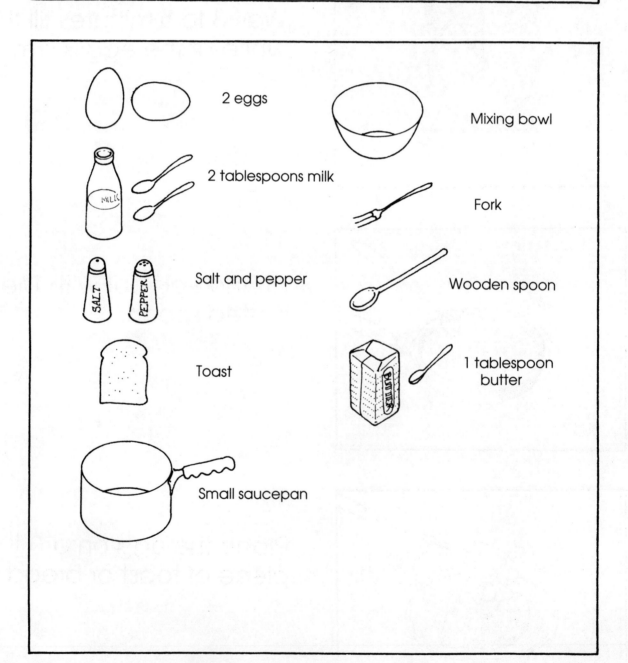

2 eggs

Mixing bowl

2 tablespoons milk

Fork

Salt and pepper

Wooden spoon

Toast

1 tablespoon butter

Small saucepan

22

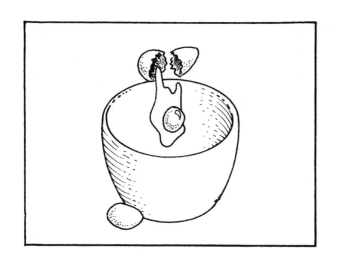

1 **Wash your hands.**

Break two eggs into the bowl.

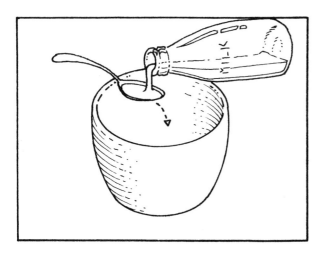

2

Add two tablespoons of milk.

3

Add a pinch of salt and pepper.

4

Beat the mixture with the fork.

5

Turn the ring on to **low**.

6

Put the butter into the saucepan.

7

Put the saucepan on the ring so the butter can melt.

8

Pour the egg mixture into the saucepan.

24

9

Keep stirring the mixture till it sets.

10

Turn the ring off.

11

Butter a piece of toast.

12

Spoon the scrambled eggs on to the toast.

Oatmeal Porridge

For 1 person

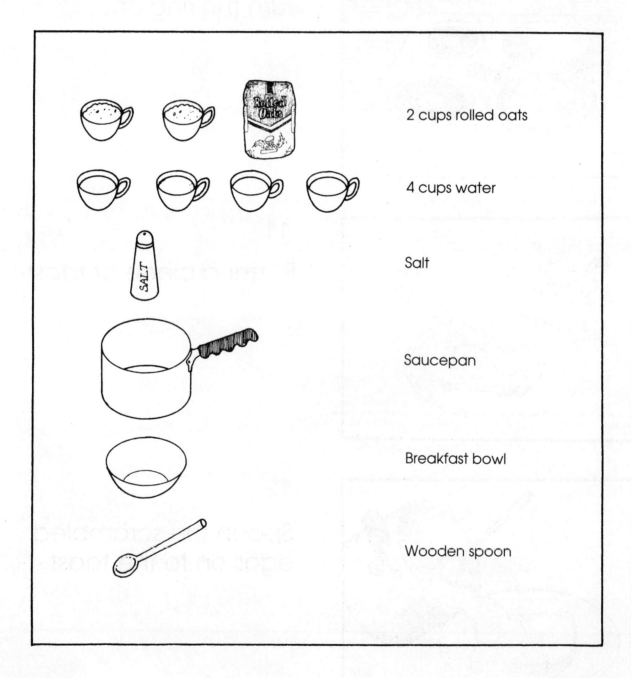

2 cups rolled oats

4 cups water

Salt

Saucepan

Breakfast bowl

Wooden spoon

26

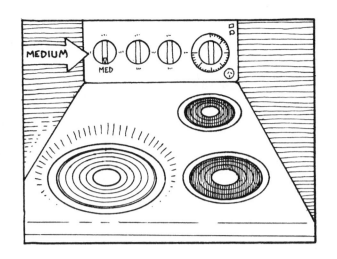

1 **Wash your hands.**

Turn the ring on to
medium.

2

Pour 4 cups of water into
the saucepan.

3

Place the saucepan on
the ring.

4

Wait 5 minutes for the
water to boil.

5

Add 2 cups of rolled oats.

6

Add a pinch of salt.

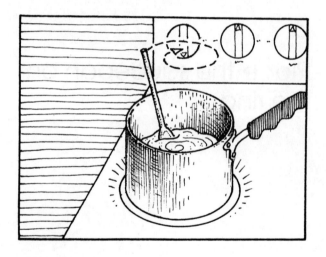

7

Stir the mixture.

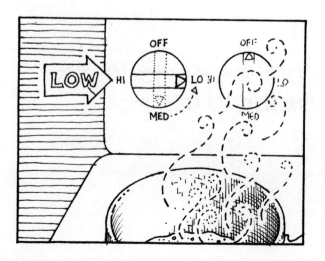

8

Turn the ring from medium to **low**.

28

9

Simmer the porridge for 20 minutes.

10

Now and again stir the porridge.

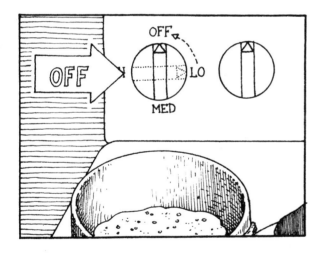

11

Turn the ring **off**.

12

Pour the porridge into the breakfast bowl.

Sausages

For 1-2 people

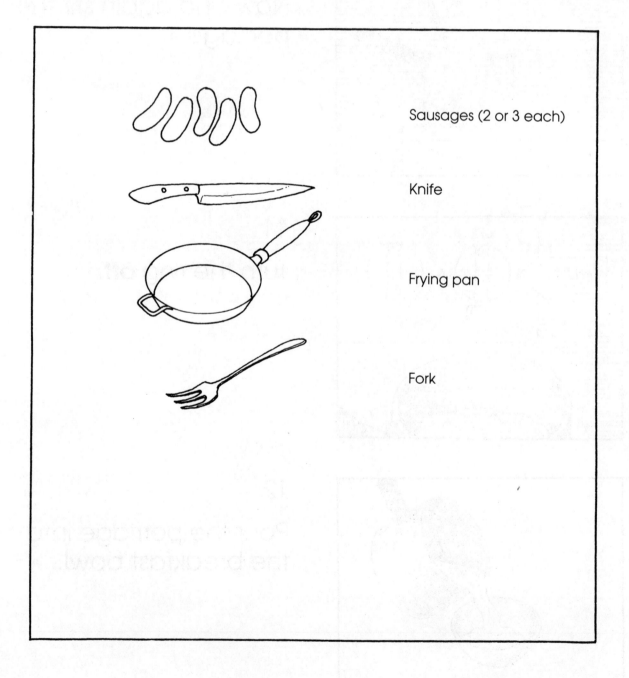

Sausages (2 or 3 each)

Knife

Frying pan

Fork

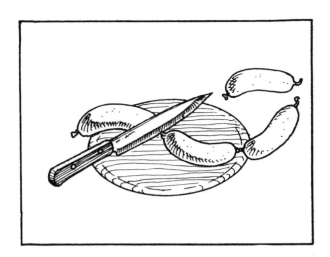

1 **Wash your hands.**

Separate the sausages with the knife.

2

Prick each sausage with the fork.

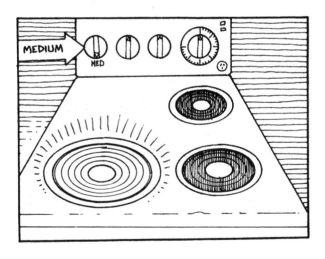

3

Turn the ring on to **medium**.

4

Put the frying pan on the ring so it can heat up.

5

Place the sausages in the frying pan.

6

Turn and roll the sausages often.

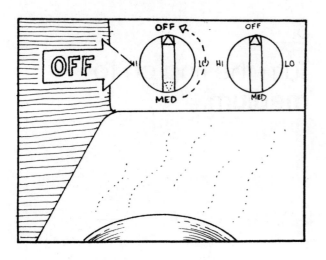

7

When the sausages are cooked, turn the ring **off**.

32

Lunch

Bacon and Egg Pie

For 4 people

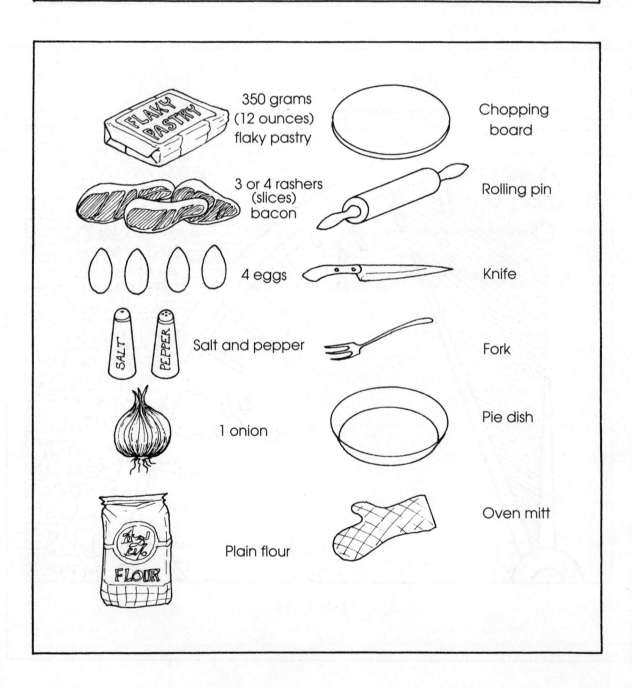

350 grams (12 ounces) flaky pastry

Chopping board

3 or 4 rashers (slices) bacon

Rolling pin

4 eggs

Knife

Salt and pepper

Fork

1 onion

Pie dish

Plain flour

Oven mitt

34

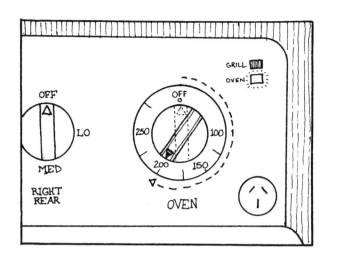

1 **Wash your hands.**

Turn the **oven** on to 200 deg. C (400 deg. F, gas mark 6).

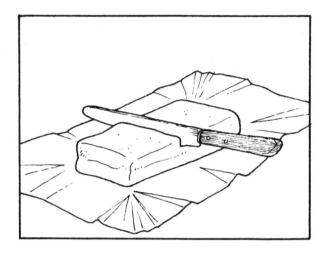

2

Divide the pastry into two halves.

3

Sprinkle flour on to the work surface and on the rolling pin.

4

Roll out half the pastry.

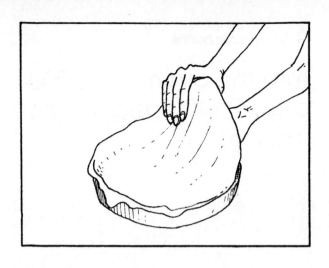

5

Put this pastry into the pie dish.

6

Chop up the bacon.

7

Sprinkle the bits of bacon on to the pastry.

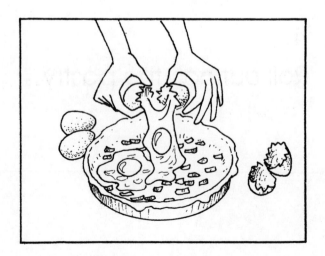

8

Break the eggs into the dish.

9

Sprinkle over a pinch of salt and pepper.

10

Peel off the skin and finely chop the onion.

11

Sprinkle the chopped onion into the dish.

12

Roll out the other half of the pastry.

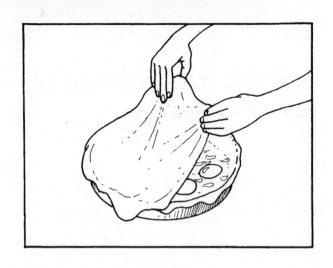

13

Put this pastry on top of the eggs, bacon, and onion.

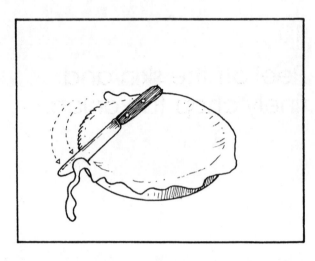

14

Cut off the edges of pastry.

15

Prick the top of the pastry with the fork.

16

Open the oven door and place the pie in the oven.

38

17

Wait 30 to 40 minutes for the pie to cook.

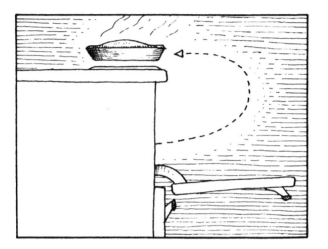

18

Take the pie out of the oven and place on top of the stove. The dish is **hot**. Use an oven mitt.

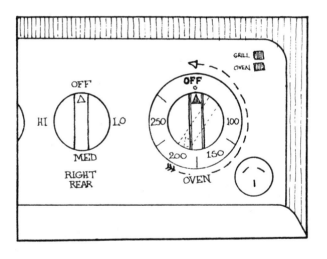

19

Turn the oven **off**.

Banana Milkshake

For 3 people

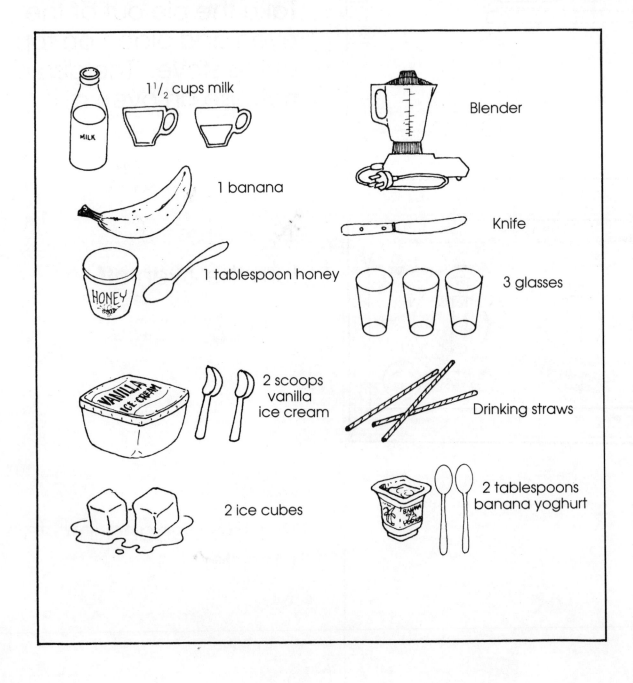

1½ cups milk

1 banana

1 tablespoon honey

2 scoops vanilla ice cream

2 ice cubes

Blender

Knife

3 glasses

Drinking straws

2 tablespoons banana yoghurt

40

1 **Wash your hands.**

Pour the milk into the blender.

2

Peel the banana.

3

Chop up the banana.

4

Put the banana into the blender.

5

Add the honey to the blender.

6

Add the banana yoghurt.

7

Add the ice cubes.

8

Add the scoops of vanilla ice-cream.

42

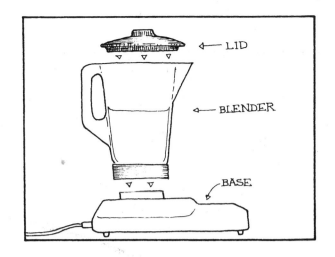

9

Put the lid on the blender. Sit the blender into the base.

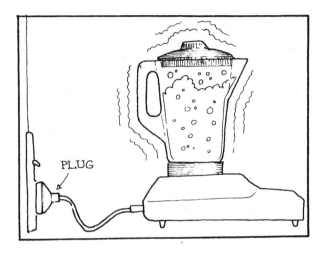

10

Turn the blender on for several minutes.

11

Pour the milkshake into 3 glasses.

12

Pop straws into the glasses.

Cheese on Toast

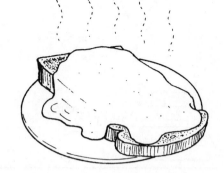

For 2 people

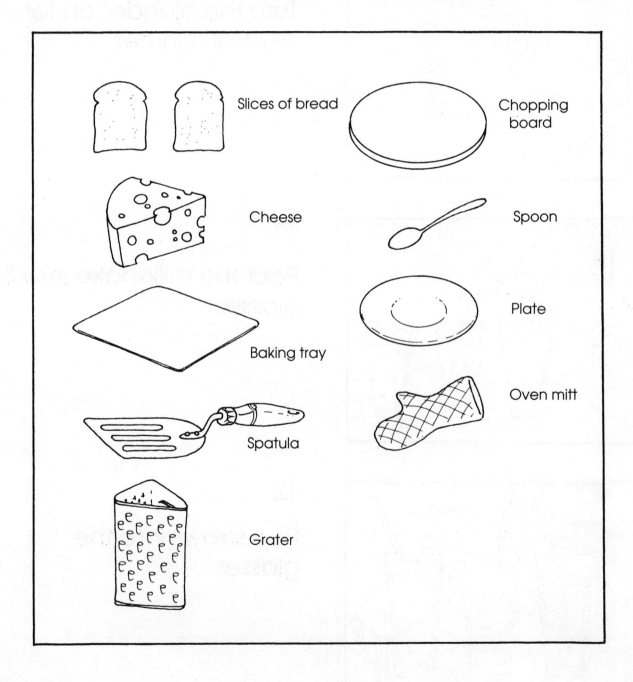

Slices of bread

Chopping board

Cheese

Spoon

Baking tray

Plate

Spatula

Oven mitt

Grater

44

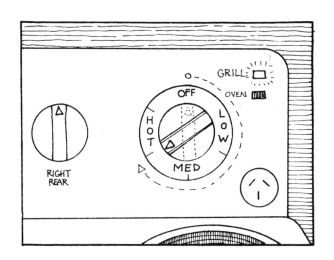

1 **Wash your hands.**

Heat the **grill** to medium hot.

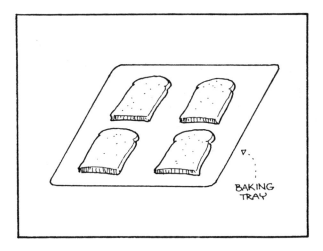

2

Place the slices of bread on the baking tray.

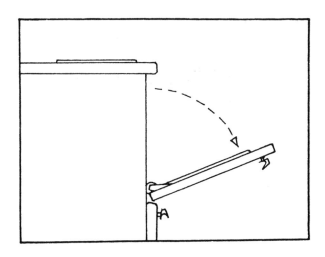

3

You may have to open the grill door.

4

Put the tray under the grill.

5

Wait 3 minutes or until the bread is **brown**.

6

Take out the tray of bread. The tray is **hot.** Use an oven mitt.

7

Turn the bread over.

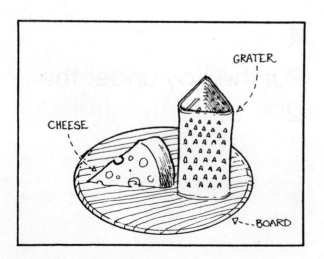

8

Find the cheese, grater, and board.

46

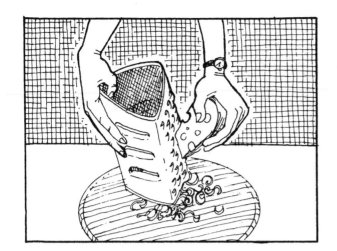

9

Grate the cheese on to the board.

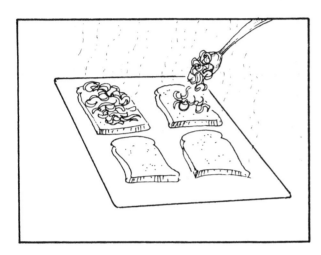

10

Place the cheese on the bread with the spoon.

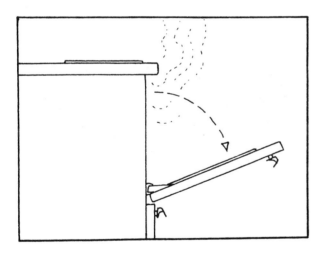

11

Open the grill door.

DON'T FORGET THE OVEN MITT

12

Place the tray under the grill. The tray is **hot**. Use an oven mitt.

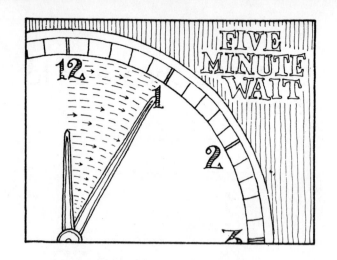

13

Wait 5 minutes or until the cheese is **brown**.

14

Take the tray out of the grill. The tray is **hot**. Use an oven mitt.

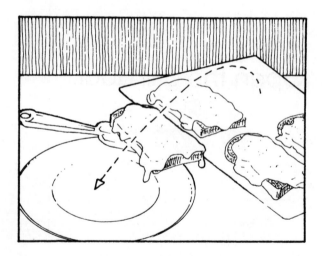

15

Place the bread with cheese on to the plate with the spatula.
Have you turned the grill off?

48

Cinnamon Toast

For 3-4 people

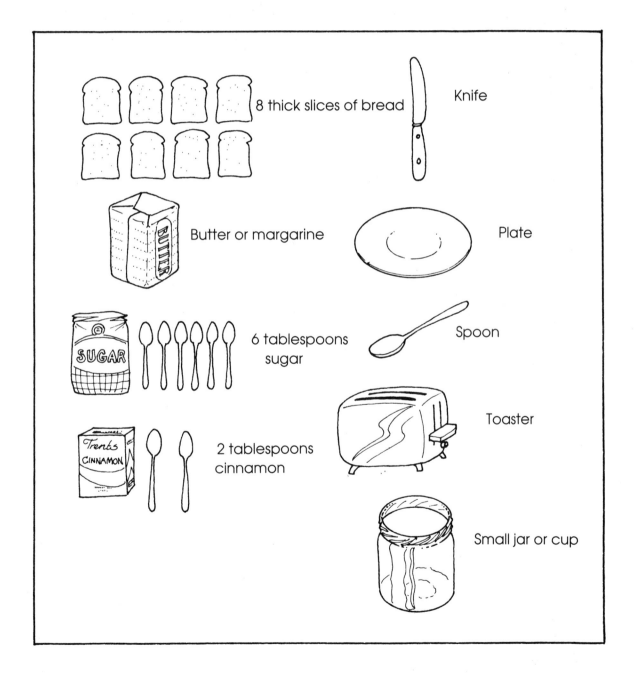

8 thick slices of bread

Knife

Butter or margarine

Plate

6 tablespoons sugar

Spoon

2 tablespoons cinnamon

Toaster

Small jar or cup

1 **Wash your hands.**

Put the sugar into a jar (or cup).

2

Add the cinnamon to the jar.

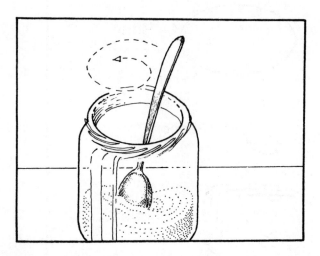

3

Stir the mixture in the jar well.

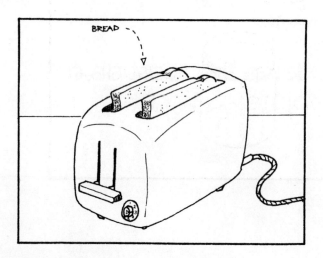

4

Put the bread into the toaster.

50

5

Butter the toast as soon as it is cooked.

6

Sprinkle the cinnamon and sugar in the jar over the toast.

7

Slice the toast with the knife.

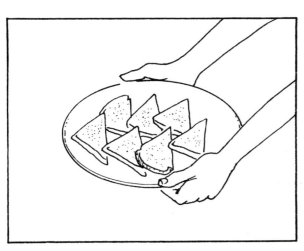

8

Serve the toast on a plate.

Hamburgers

For 4 people

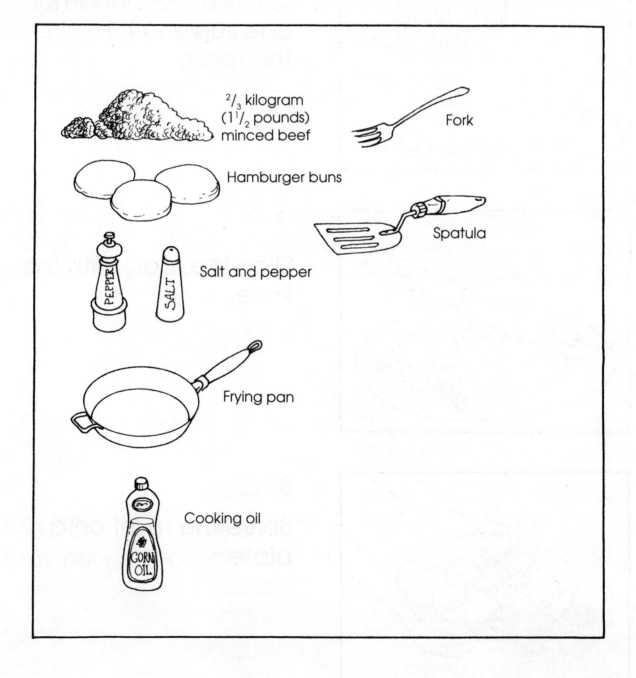

$^2/_3$ kilogram
($1^1/_2$ pounds)
minced beef

Fork

Hamburger buns

Spatula

Salt and pepper

Frying pan

Cooking oil

CORN OIL

52

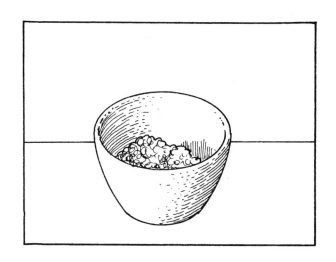

1 **Wash your hands.**

Put the minced beef in the bowl.

2

Break up the minced beef with the fork.

3

Add a pinch of salt and pepper.

4

Divide the minced beef up into patties with your hands.

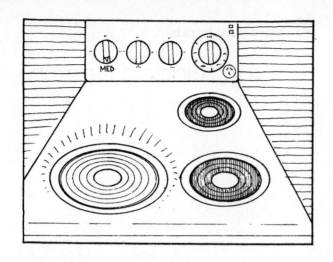

5

Turn the ring on to **medium**.

6

Place the frying pan on the ring.

7

Put a little cooking oil into the frying pan to give a thin layer on the bottom.

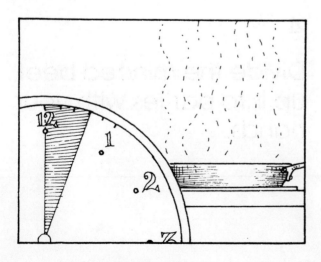

8

Heat the oil for 3 minutes.

54

9

Put the patties of mince into the frying pan.

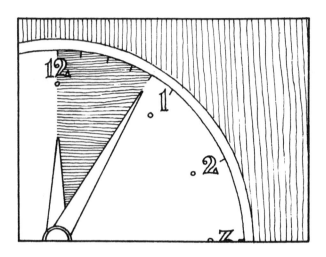

10

Wait for 4 minutes or until the patties are brown.

11

Turn the patties over with the spatula.

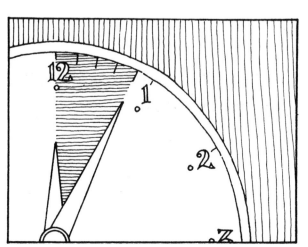

12

Wait 4 minutes or until the patties are brown.

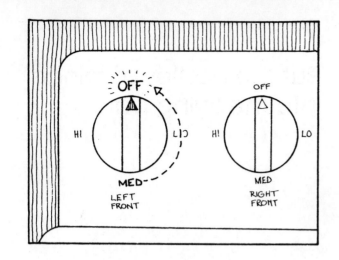

13

Turn the ring **off**.

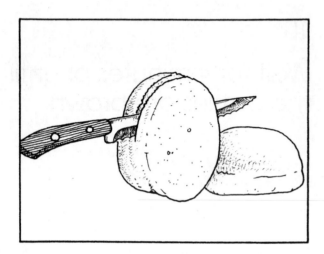

14

Cut the hamburger buns in half.

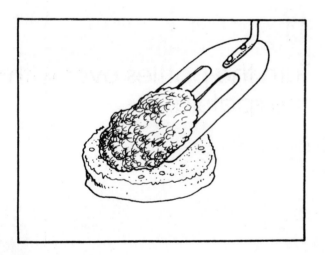

15

Place the hamburger patty on to the bun using the spatula.

16

Cover the patty with the top of the bun.

56

Hot Dogs

For 3 people

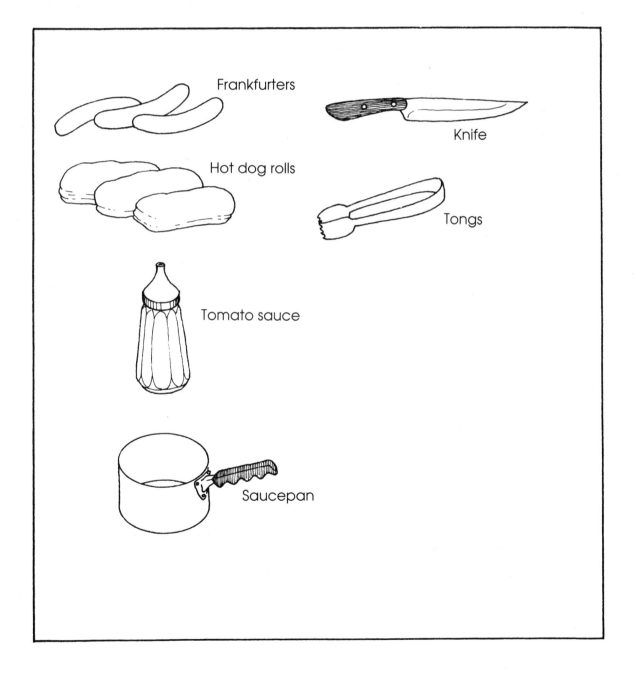

Frankfurters

Knife

Hot dog rolls

Tongs

Tomato sauce

Saucepan

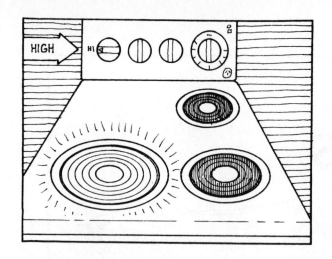

1 **Wash your hands.**

Turn the ring on to **high**.

2

Half-fill the saucepan with water.

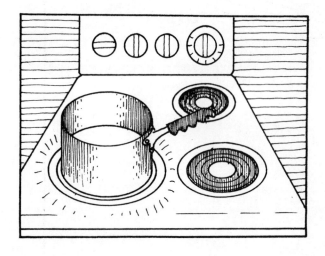

3

Place the saucepan on the ring.

4

Wait 5 minutes for the water to boil.

5

Carefully put the frankfurters into the boiling water using the tongs.

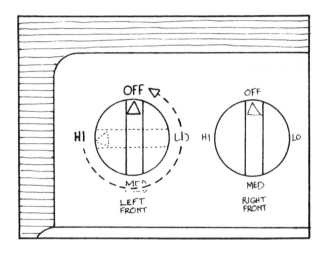

6

Turn the ring **off**.

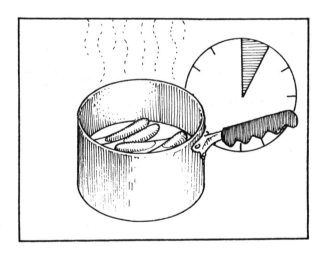

7

Leave the frankfurters in the hot water for 5 minutes.

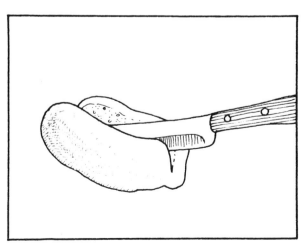

8

Slit open the side of each hot dog roll.

9

Using tongs, take the frankfurters out of the saucepan.

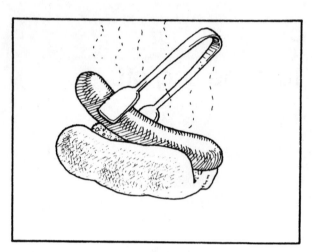

10

Place a frankfurter inside each roll.

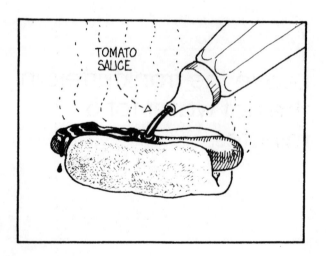

11

Put some tomato sauce on to the frankfurter.

60

Omelette

For 1 person

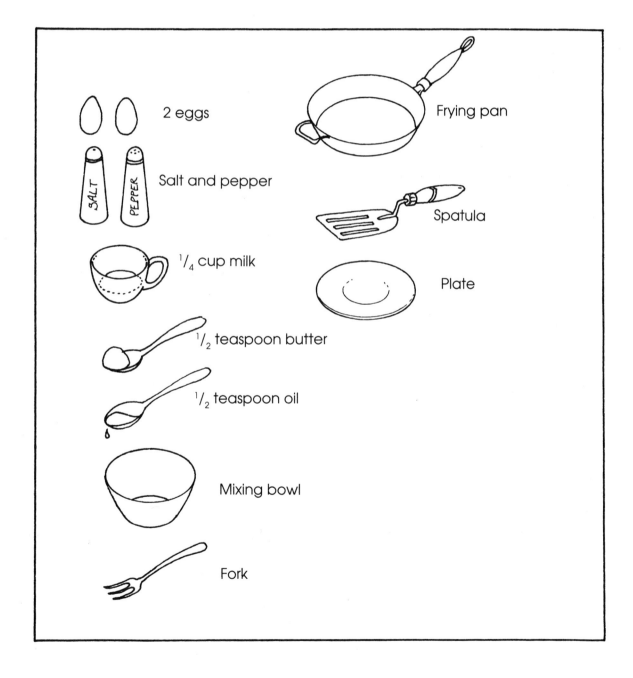

2 eggs

Salt and pepper

$\frac{1}{4}$ cup milk

$\frac{1}{2}$ teaspoon butter

$\frac{1}{2}$ teaspoon oil

Mixing bowl

Fork

Frying pan

Spatula

Plate

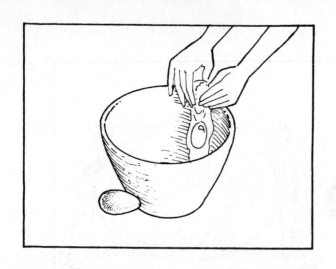

1 **Wash your hands.**

Break the eggs into the bowl.

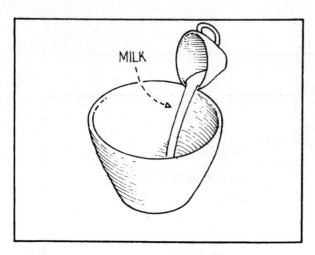

MILK

2

Add the milk.

SALT PEPPER

3

Add a pinch of salt and pepper.

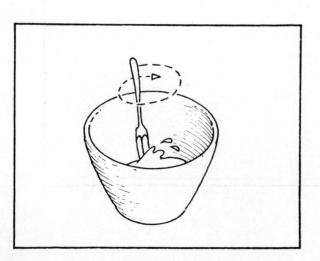

4

Lightly mix with the fork.

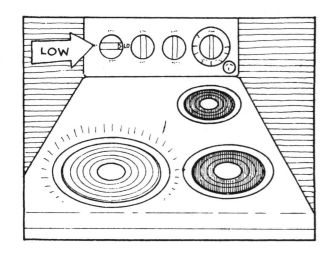

5

Turn the ring on to **low**.

6

Add the butter and the oil to the frying pan.

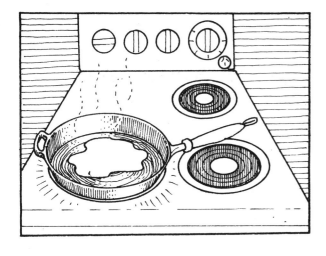

7

Melt the butter and oil on the stove.

8

Add the egg mixture.

9

Place the lid on the frying pan.

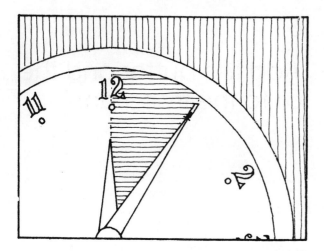

10

Wait five minutes.

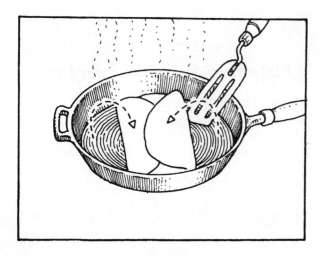

11

Flip the outside edges into the centre.

12

Place the omelette on to a plate with the spatula. Have you turned the ring off?

64

Pancakes

For 1 person

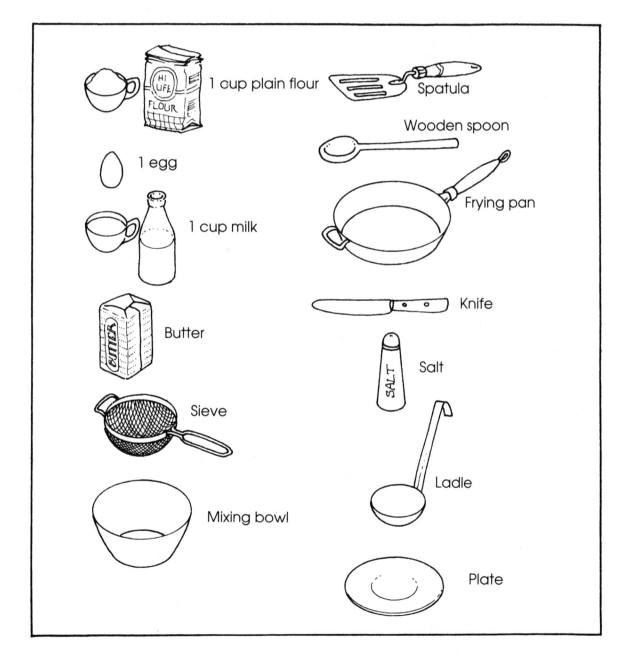

1 cup plain flour

1 egg

1 cup milk

Butter

Sieve

Mixing bowl

Spatula

Wooden spoon

Frying pan

Knife

Salt

Ladle

Plate

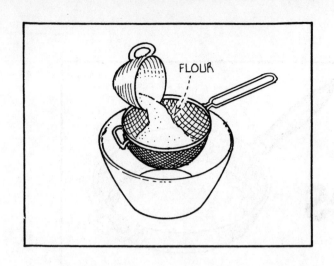

1 **Wash your hands.**

Sift the plain flour into the bowl.

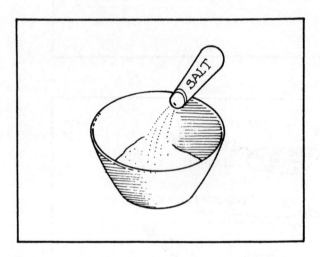

2

Add a pinch of salt.

3

Drop the egg into the flour and salt.

4

Add the milk gradually.

66

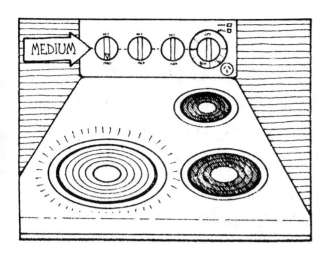

5

Turn the ring on to **medium**.

6

Put a little butter into the frying pan.

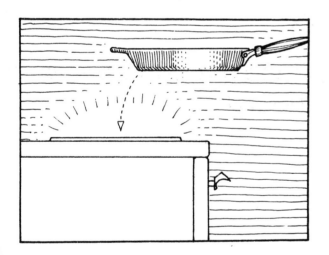

7

Put the frying pan on the ring so the butter can melt.

8

When the butter has melted, put a ladle full of mixture into the frying pan. Swish it around to cover the pan.

9

When you see air bubbles come to the surface, turn the pancake with the spatula and cook the other side.

10

If you dare, flip the pancake in the air back on to the other side!

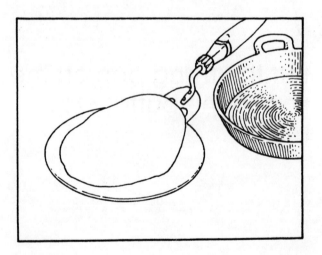

11

Place the pancake on to the plate.

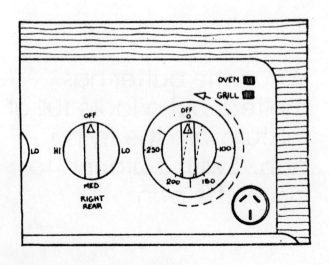

12

Turn the ring **off**.

Pizza Snacks

For 2 people

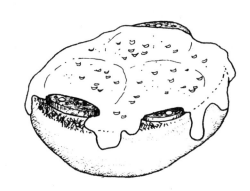

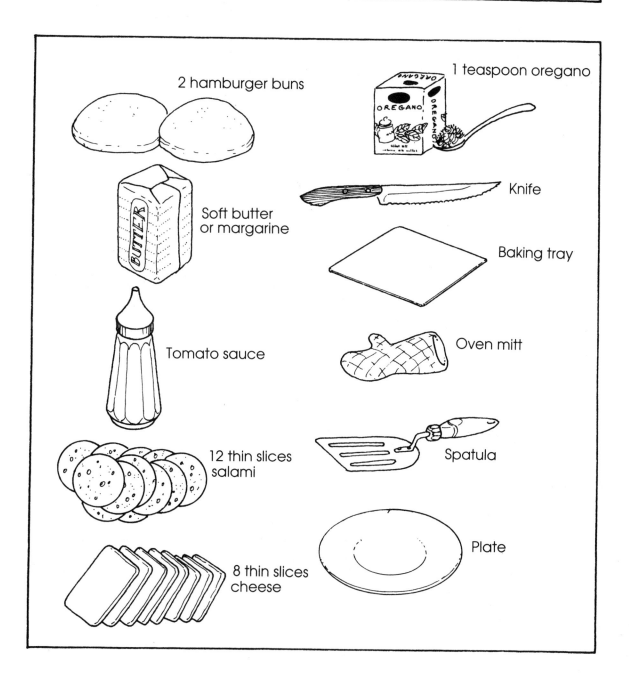

2 hamburger buns

1 teaspoon oregano

Soft butter or margarine

Knife

Baking tray

Tomato sauce

Oven mitt

12 thin slices salami

Spatula

8 thin slices cheese

Plate

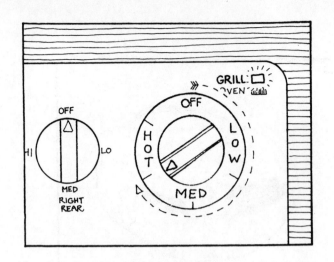

1 **Wash your hands.**

Turn the **grill** to medium hot.

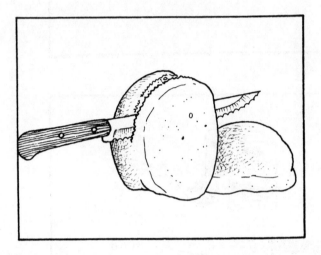

2

Cut the hamburger buns in half.

3

Butter the bun halves.

4

Place the hamburger buns on the baking tray.

70

5

Put the tray under the grill until the buns start to go brown.

6

Take the tray out of the grill. The tray is **hot**. Use an oven mitt.

TOMATO SAUCE

7

Spread tomato sauce on the bun halves.

8

Place 3 slices of salami on each bun half.

9

Put 2 slices of cheese on top of each bun half.

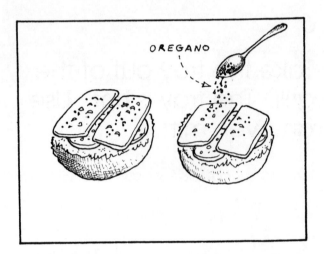

10

Sprinkle a little oregano on top.

11

Put the baking tray back under the grill till the cheese melts. The tray is **hot**. Use an oven mitt.

12

Place the snacks on to the plate with the spatula.

Have you turned the grill off?

Savoury Snacks

For 2 people

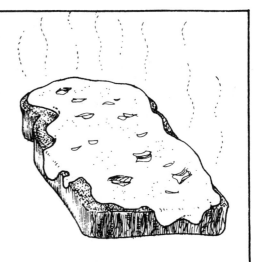

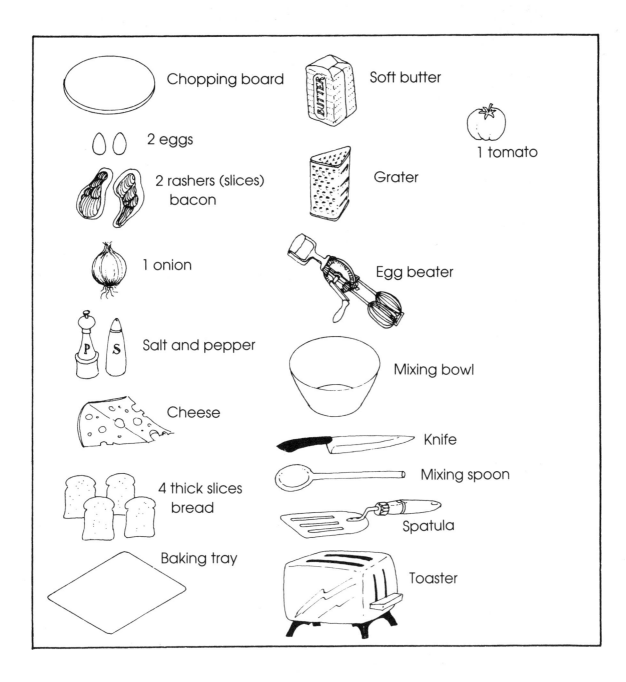

Chopping board

2 eggs

2 rashers (slices) bacon

1 onion

Salt and pepper

Cheese

4 thick slices bread

Baking tray

Soft butter

1 tomato

Grater

Egg beater

Mixing bowl

Knife

Mixing spoon

Spatula

Toaster

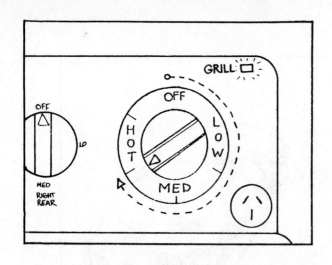

1 **Wash your hands.**

Turn the **grill** on to medium hot.

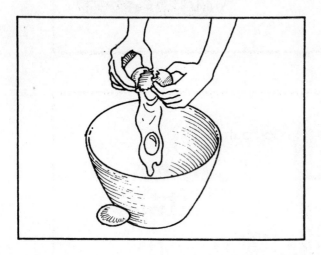

2

Break the eggs into the bowl.

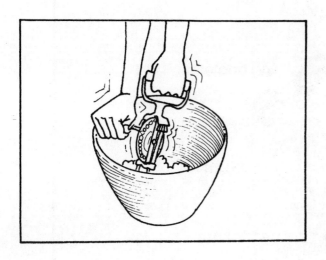

3

Beat the eggs with an egg beater.

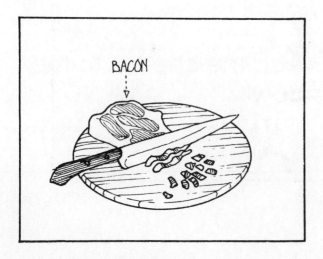

BACON

4

Chop the bacon into small bits.

74

5

Chop the tomato into small bits.

6

Scrape the tomato and bacon bits into the bowl.

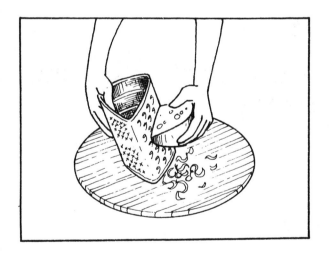

7

Grate enough cheese to fill one cup.

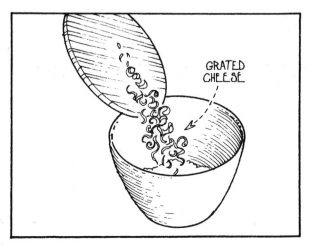

8

Add the cheese to the bowl.

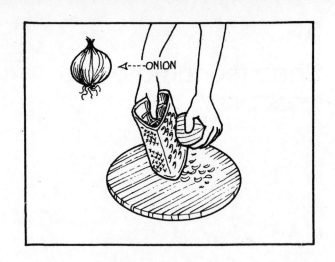

9

Peel an onion. Grate the onion.

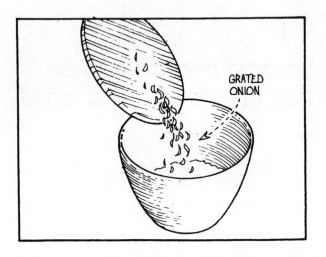

10

Add the onion to the bowl.

11

Add a pinch of salt and pepper.

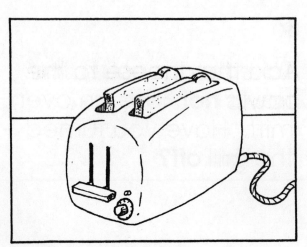

12

Lightly toast the bread.

13

Butter each slice of toast.

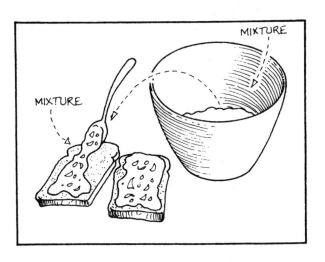

14

Spread the mixture on each slice of toast with the spoon.

15

Place the snacks on to the baking tray. Place the baking tray under the grill till the snacks are golden.

16

Take the tray out. The tray is **hot**. Use an oven mitt. Have you turned the grill **off?**

Pumpkin Soup

For 1-2 people

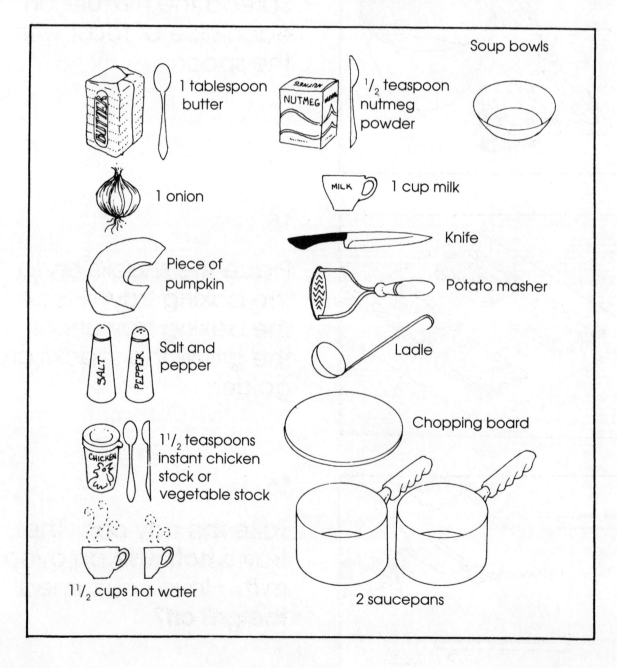

1 tablespoon butter

1 onion

Piece of pumpkin

Salt and pepper

$1\frac{1}{2}$ teaspoons instant chicken stock or vegetable stock

$1\frac{1}{2}$ cups hot water

$\frac{1}{2}$ teaspoon nutmeg powder

1 cup milk

Soup bowls

Knife

Potato masher

Ladle

Chopping board

2 saucepans

78

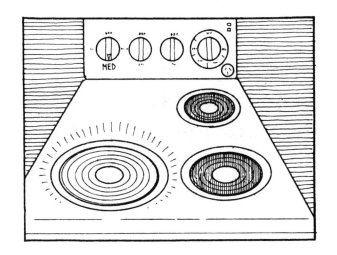

1 **Wash your hands.**

Turn the ring on to **medium**.

2

Half-fill one of the saucepans with water.

3

Boil the water on the ring.

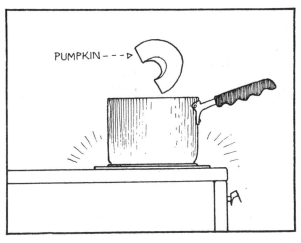

4

Peel the pumpkin piece and remove the seeds. Put the pumpkin in the pan.

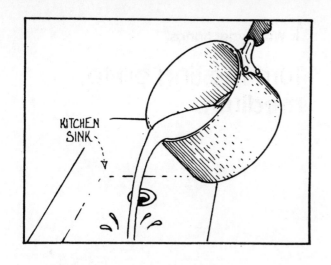

5

When the pumpkin is soft, **carefully** pour off most of the hot water using the sieve.

6

Mash the pumpkin with the potato masher.

7

Place the butter into the clean saucepan.

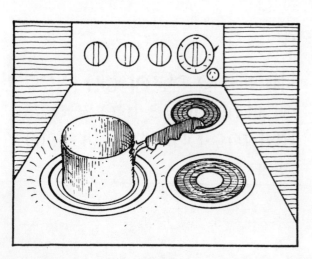

8

Put the saucepan on the ring and melt the butter.

9

Peel an onion and chop it up.

10

Add the onion to the butter in the saucepan.

11

Fry the onion till it is golden.

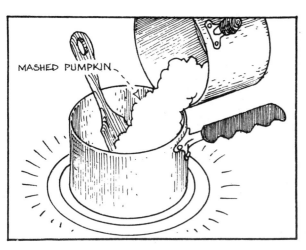

12

Stir in the mashed pumpkin.

13

Add a pinch of salt and pepper.

14

Stir the chicken (or vegetable) stock into the cup of water.

15

Add the cup of stock to the saucepan.

16

Add the nutmeg.

82

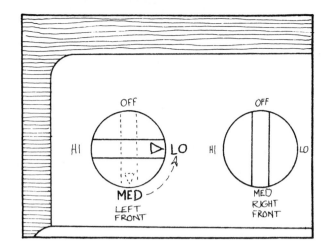

17

Turn the heat from medium to **low**. Simmer for five minutes.

18

Stir in the cup of milk.

19

Heat the soup until it is almost boiling.

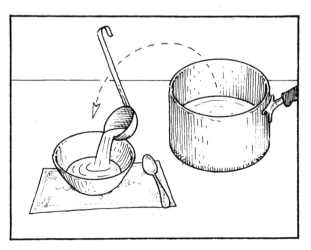

20

Carefully put the soup into the soup bowls with the ladle.
Have you turned the ring off?

84

Dinner

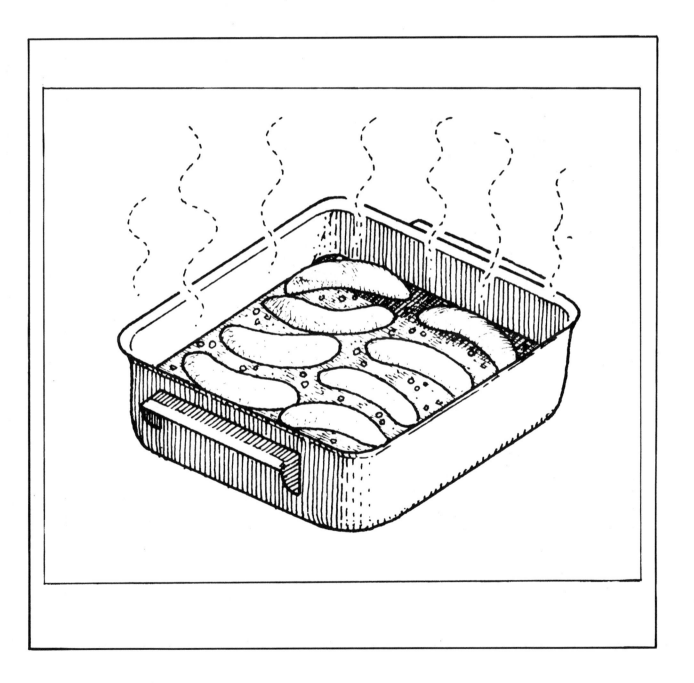

Beans

For 2-4 people

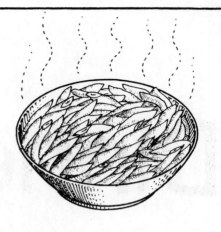

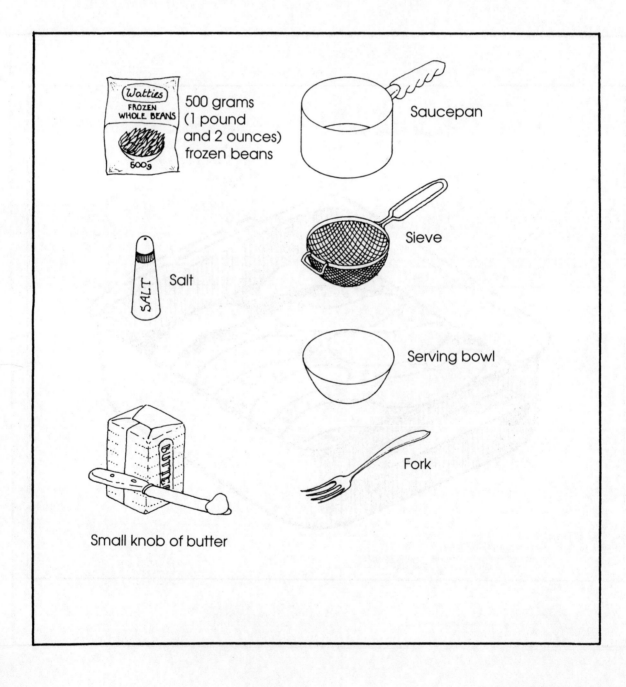

500 grams
(1 pound
and 2 ounces)
frozen beans

Saucepan

Salt

Sieve

Serving bowl

Fork

Small knob of butter

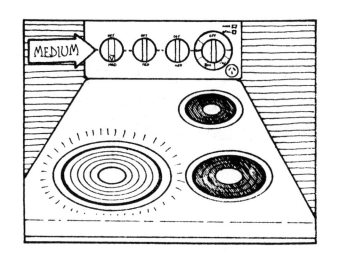

1 **Wash your hands.**

Turn the ring on to **medium.**

2

Half-fill the saucepan with water.

3

Place the saucepan on to the ring.

4

Wait 5 minutes for the water to boil.

5

Pour the frozen beans into the boiling water. Add a pinch of salt.

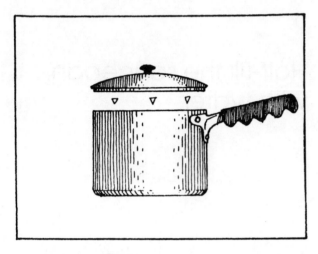

6

Put the lid on the saucepan.

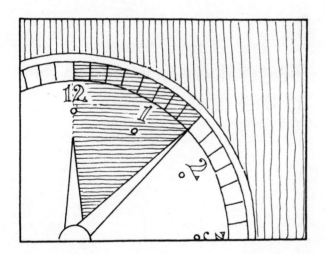

7

Wait 8 minutes for the beans to boil.

8

Put a bean on to the fork and let it cool.

88

9

Put the bean into your mouth. It may still be **hot.**

10

If the bean is **hard**, boil the beans a little longer.

11

If the bean is soft, tip the beans into the sieve.

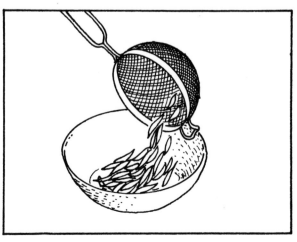

12

Put the beans into the bowl.

13

Add a knob of butter.

14

Gently stir the beans.

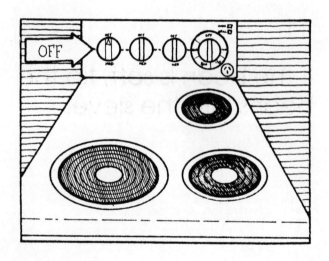

15

Did you remember to turn off the ring?

Carrots

For 2-4 people

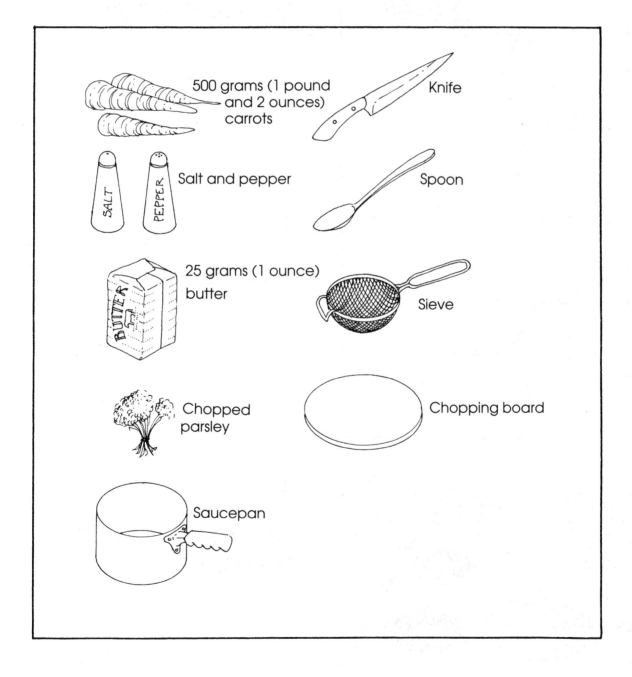

500 grams (1 pound and 2 ounces) carrots

Knife

Salt and pepper

Spoon

25 grams (1 ounce) butter

Sieve

Chopped parsley

Chopping board

Saucepan

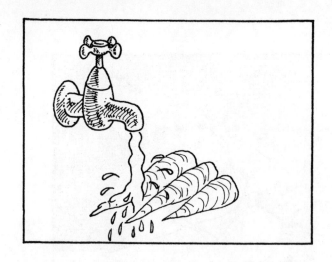

1 Wash your hands.

Wash the carrots.

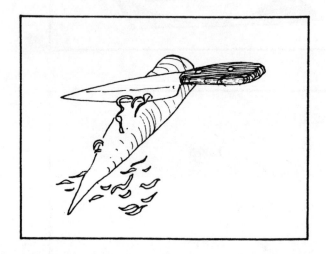

2

Scrape the carrots.

3

Slice the carrots into thin rings.

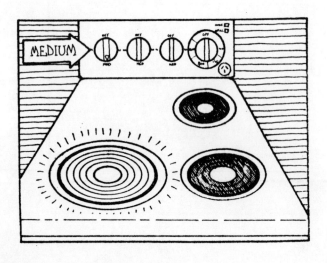

4

Turn the ring on to **medium**.

92

5

Half-fill the saucepan
with water.

6

Place the saucepan on
the ring.

7

Wait 5 minutes for the
water to boil.

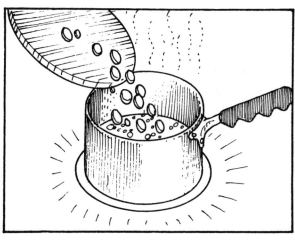

8

Add the carrot rings.

9

Add a pinch of salt.

10

Put the lid on the saucepan.

11

Wait 15 minutes for the carrots to soften.

12

Drain the cooked carrots.
Turn the ring **off**.

13

Add the butter.

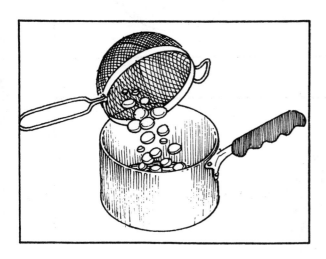

14

Return the drained carrots back to the saucepan.

15

Add a pinch of pepper and the chopped parsley.

16

Gently stir the carrots.

Coleslaw

For 2-4 people

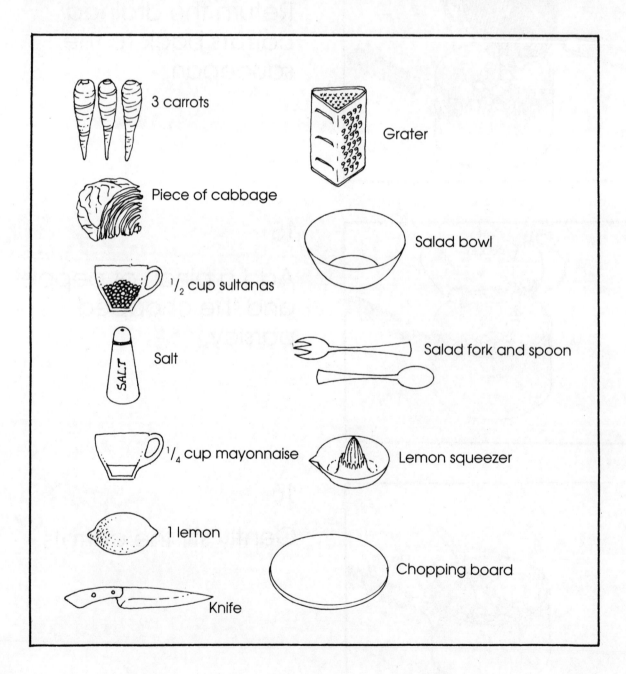

3 carrots

Grater

Piece of cabbage

Salad bowl

1/2 cup sultanas

Salt

Salad fork and spoon

1/4 cup mayonnaise

Lemon squeezer

1 lemon

Chopping board

Knife

96

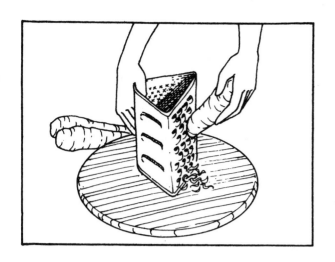

1 **Wash your hands.**

Grate the carrots.

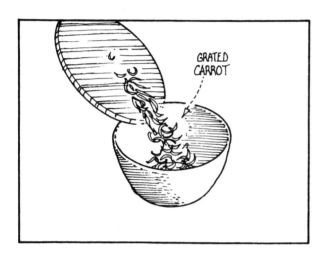

GRATED CARROT

2

Put the carrots in the salad bowl.

CABBAGE.

3

Slice the piece of cabbage on the chopping board.

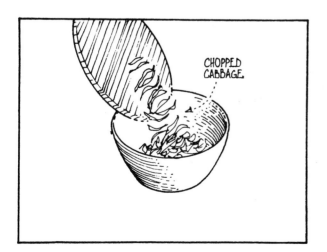

CHOPPED CABBAGE.

4

Put the sliced cabbage in the salad bowl.

5

Put $\frac{1}{2}$ cup sultanas in the bowl.

6

Put a pinch of salt in the bowl.

7

Mix with the salad fork and spoon.

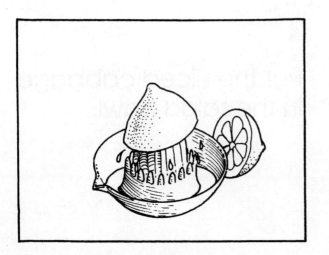

8

Cut the lemon into two pieces. Squeeze out the juice.

9

Pour the juice into the bowl.

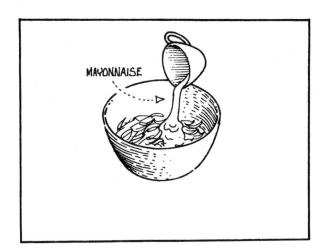

10

Pour the mayonnaise into the bowl.

11

Mix with the salad fork and spoon.

Peas

For 2-4 people

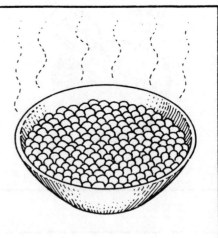

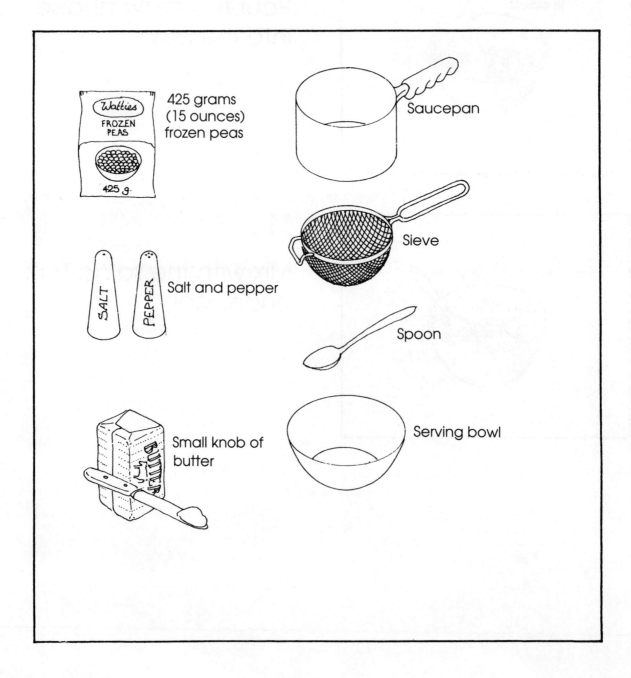

425 grams (15 ounces) frozen peas

Saucepan

Sieve

Salt and pepper

Spoon

Small knob of butter

Serving bowl

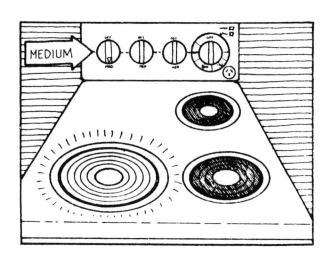

1 **Wash your hands.**

Turn the ring onto **medium**.

2

Half-fill the saucepan with water.

3

Place the saucepan on the ring.

4

Wait 5 minutes for the water to boil.

5

Add the peas.

6

Put the lid on the saucepan.

7

Wait 5 minutes for the peas to boil.

8

Put a pea on to a spoon and let it cool.

9

Put the pea into your mouth. It may still be **hot.**

10

If the pea is **hard**, boil the peas a little longer.

11

If the pea is **soft**, tip the peas into the sieve. Have you turned the ring off?

12

Put the peas into the bowl.

13

Add a knob of butter.

14

Add a pinch of salt and pepper.

15

Gently stir the peas.

Potato Salad

For 4 people

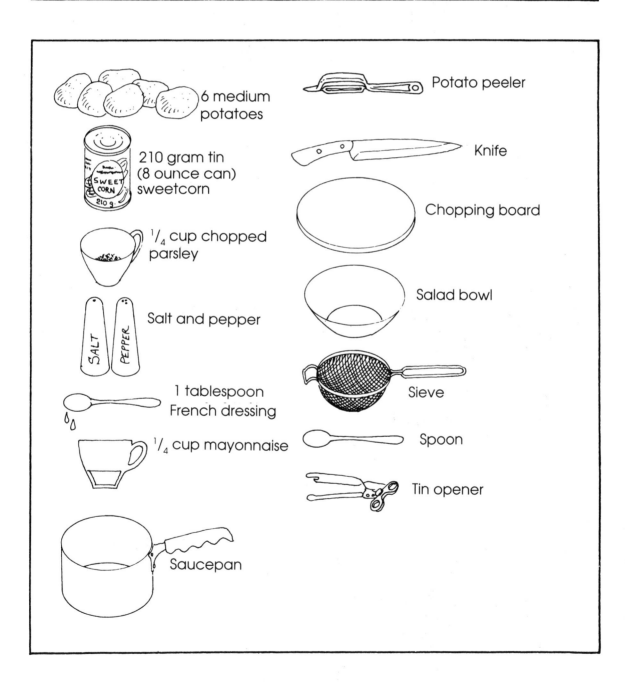

6 medium potatoes

210 gram tin (8 ounce can) sweetcorn

$1/4$ cup chopped parsley

Salt and pepper

1 tablespoon French dressing

$1/4$ cup mayonnaise

Saucepan

Potato peeler

Knife

Chopping board

Salad bowl

Sieve

Spoon

Tin opener

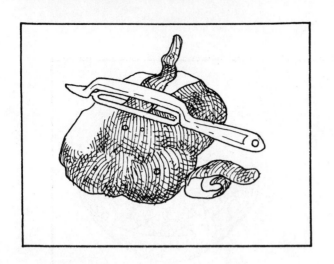

1 **Wash your hands.**

Peel the skins off the potatoes with the potato peeler.

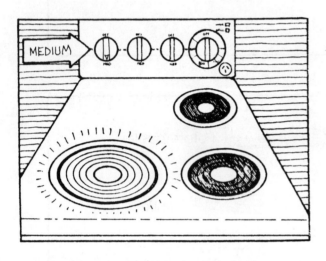

2

Turn the ring on to **medium**.

3

Half-fill the saucepan with water.

4

Add a pinch of salt to the water.

5

Cut the potatoes into even-sized pieces.

POTATO PIECES

6

Carefully add the potatoes to the water in the saucepan.

7

Put the saucepan on the ring.

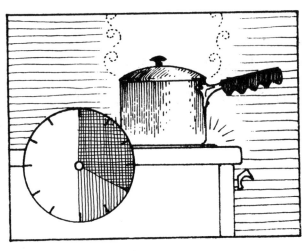

8

Simmer for 20-30 minutes till the potatoes are tender.

9

Carefully drain the potatoes using the sieve. Turn off the ring.

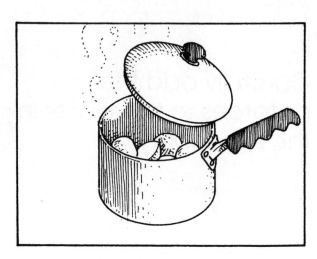

10

Put the potatoes back in the saucepan. Leave the lid off the saucepan so the potatoes can cool.

11

When cool, cut the potatoes into cubes.

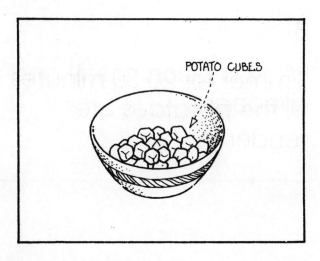

POTATO CUBES

12

Put the potato cubes into the salad bowl.

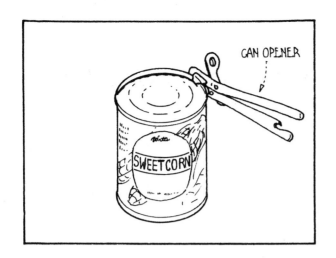

13

Open the tin of sweetcorn with the tin opener.

14

Pour the sweetcorn into the sieve so it can drain.

15

Pour the sweetcorn into the bowl of potato cubes.

16

Add a pinch of salt and pepper.

17

Add the chopped parsley.

18

Add the French dressing.

19

Add the mayonnaise.

20

Gently mix it all together. Serve cold.

Mashed Potatoes

For 4-6 people

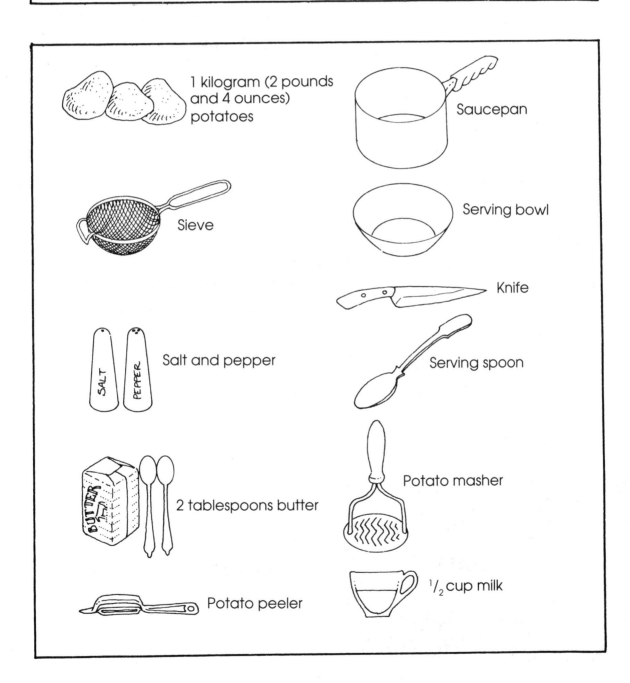

1 kilogram (2 pounds and 4 ounces) potatoes

Saucepan

Sieve

Serving bowl

Knife

Salt and pepper

Serving spoon

2 tablespoons butter

Potato masher

Potato peeler

1/2 cup milk

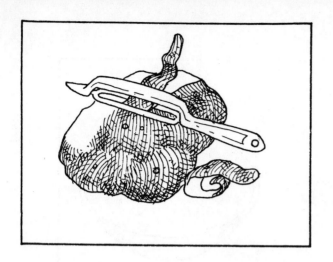

1 **Wash your hands.**

Peel the skins off the potatoes with the potato peeler.

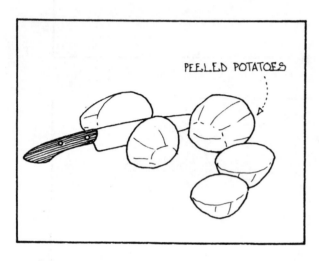

PEELED POTATOES

2

Cut the potatoes into even-sized pieces.

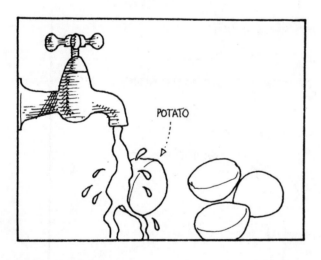

POTATO

3

Wash the potatoes under cold water.

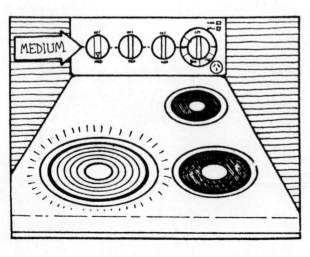

MEDIUM

4

Turn the ring on to **medium**.

112

5

Half-fill the saucepan with hot water.

6

Add a pinch of salt to the hot water.

7

Place the saucepan on the ring.

8

Wait 5 minutes for the water to boil

9

Add the potatoes carefully when the water has boiled.

10

Put the lid on the saucepan.

11

Simmer for 20-30 minutes till the potatoes are fairly soft. Turn the ring **off**.

12

Carefully drain the potatoes using the sieve. Put them back in the saucepan.

114

13

Add the milk.

14

Add the butter and a pinch of pepper.

15

Put the lid back on for a minute.

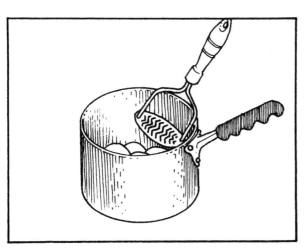

16

Mash the potatoes well with the potato masher till the potatoes are smooth and there are NO lumps.

17

Stir the mashed potatoes
with the serving spoon
for extra smoothness.

18

Put the mashed potato
into the serving bowl
using the serving spoon.

Rice

For 2 people

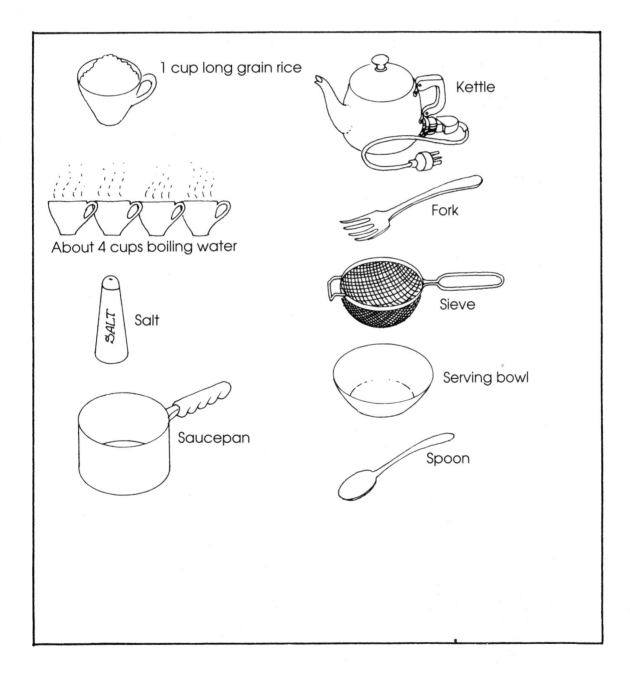

1 cup long grain rice

Kettle

About 4 cups boiling water

Fork

Salt

Sieve

Serving bowl

Saucepan

Spoon

1 Wash your hands.

Put the rice into the saucepan.

2

Cover the rice with cold water.

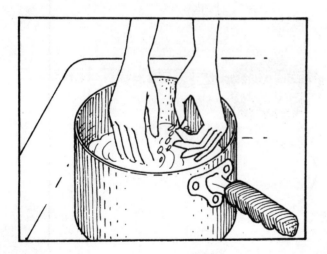

3

Wash the rice by rubbing it between your fingers.

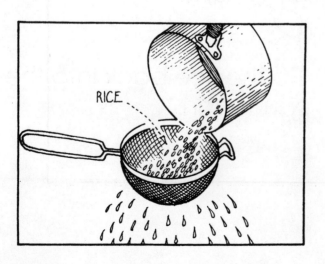

RICE

4

Carefully pour off the cloudy water using the sieve. Put the rice back into the saucepan.

118

5

Cover the rice again with cold water.

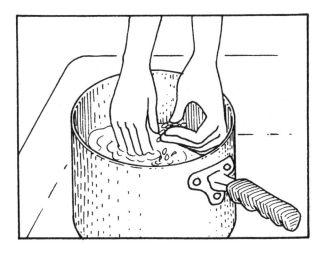

6

Again wash the rice by rubbing it between your fingers.

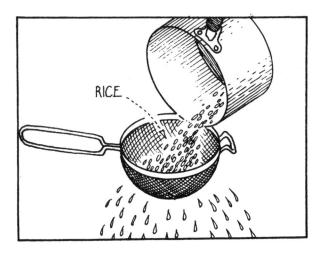

RICE

7

Carefully pour off the cloudy water again using the sieve.

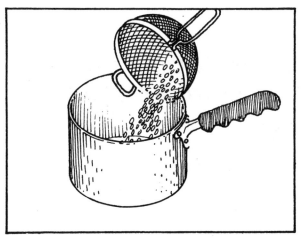

8

Tip the rice back into the saucepan.

9

Put water into the kettle.

10

Plug the kettle into the socket so the water can boil. Switch off the kettle when it has boiled.

11

Use a cup to measure the boiling water.

12

Carefully pour 4 cups of boiling water over the rice.

13

Sprinkle a pinch of salt over the rice.

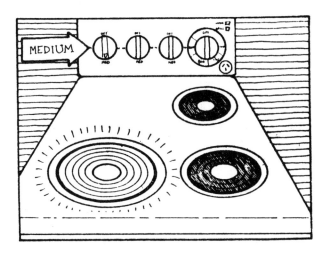

14

Turn the ring on to **medium**.

15

Place the saucepan on to the ring.

16

Boil the rice for 8-10 minutes.

17

Stir the rice now and again with the fork.

RICE.

18

Put some rice into your mouth to test that it is cooked. The rice is **hot**.

19

When cooked, tip the rice into the sieve. **Have you turned the ring off?**

20

Tip the rice into the bowl.

Chicken

For 4 people

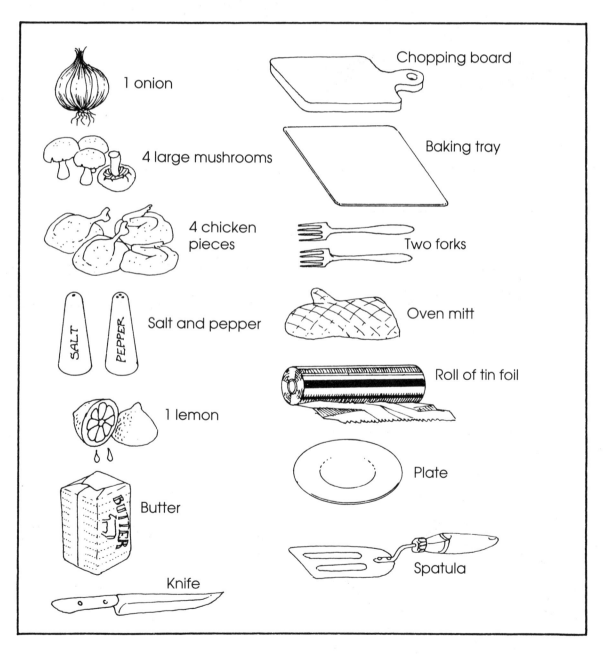

1 onion

Chopping board

4 large mushrooms

Baking tray

4 chicken pieces

Two forks

Salt and pepper

Oven mitt

1 lemon

Roll of tin foil

Butter

Plate

Knife

Spatula

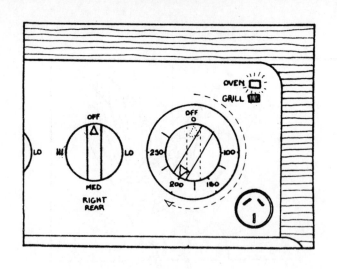

1 **Wash your hands.**

Turn the oven on to 200 deg. C (400 deg. F, gas mark 6).

2

Chop up the mushrooms.

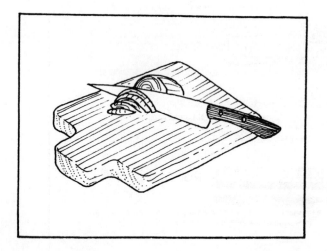

3

Peel off the skin and finely chop up the onion.

4

Rip off 4 squares of tin foil.

124

5

Place each chicken piece in the centre of a piece of foil.

6

Put some mushrooms and onions on top of the chicken.

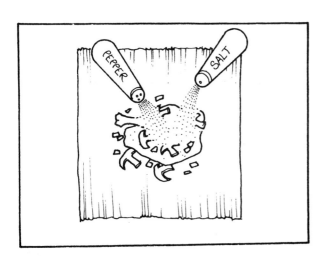

7

Sprinkle a pinch of salt and pepper over the chicken.

8

Squeeze some lemon juice over the chicken.

9

Put a knob of butter on the chicken.

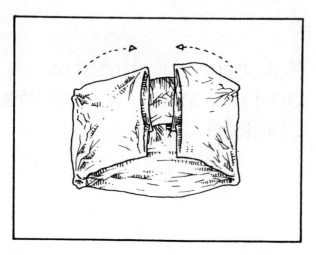

10

Fold up the foil - like a parcel - sealing the edges well.

11

Put the 4 parcels of chicken on to the baking tray.

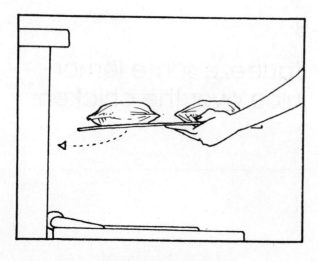

12

Open the oven door and put the tray into the oven.

126

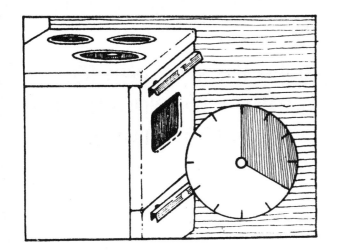

13

Bake the parcels of chicken for 20 minutes.

14

Open the oven door and place the tray on top of the stove. The tray is **hot.** Use an oven mitt.

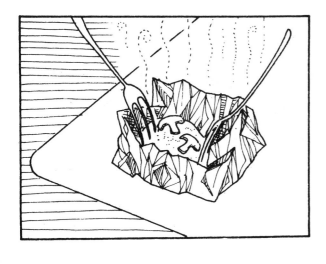

15

Carefully open the foil with 2 forks.

16

Put the open parcels of chicken back into the oven. Use and oven mitt.

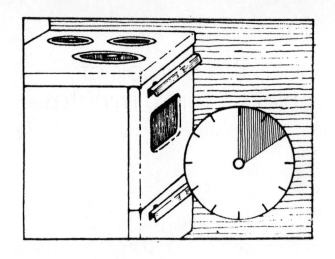

17

Bake the chicken for another 10 minutes. This browns the chicken.

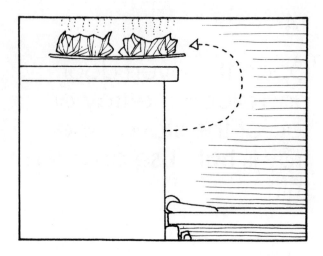

18

After 10 minutes, put the tray on top of the stove. The tray is **hot.** Use an oven mitt.

19

Lift the chicken from the tray on to a plate with the 2 forks.

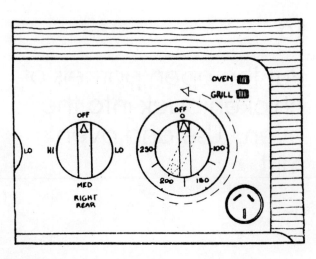

20

Turn the oven **off.**

Meat Loaf

For 4-6 people

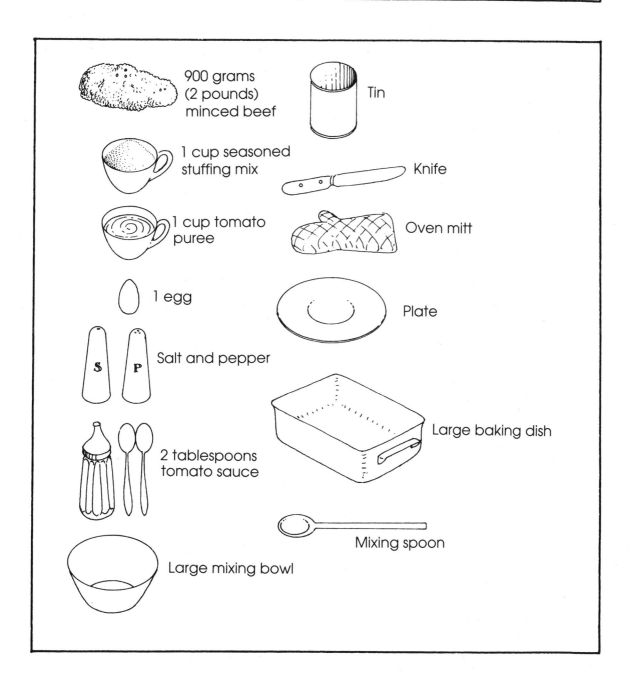

900 grams (2 pounds) minced beef

1 cup seasoned stuffing mix

1 cup tomato puree

1 egg

Salt and pepper

2 tablespoons tomato sauce

Large mixing bowl

Tin

Knife

Oven mitt

Plate

Large baking dish

Mixing spoon

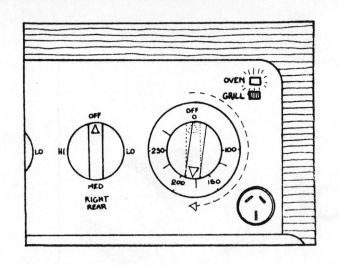

1 **Wash your hands.**

Turn the oven on to 180 deg. C (350 deg. F, gas mark 4).

2

Put the minced beef into the large mixing bowl.

3

Add the seasoned stuffing mix to the bowl.

4

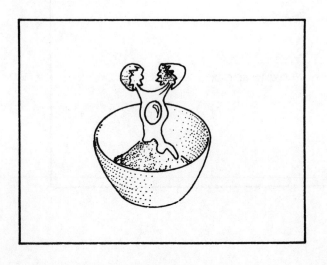

Add 1 egg.

5

Add a pinch of salt and pepper.

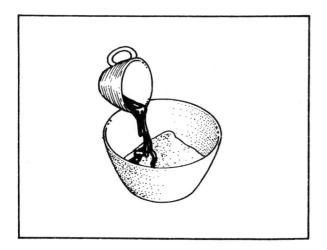

6

Add the cup of tomato puree.

7

Mix it all together, stirring well till it is mixed and smooth.

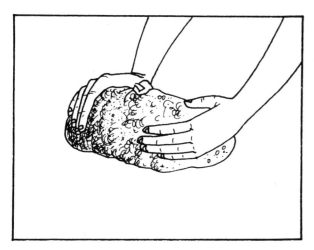

8

With clean hands, shape the mixture firmly into a loaf.

9

Put the loaf into a large baking dish.

10

Open the oven door and place the baking dish into the oven. Bake the loaf for one hour.

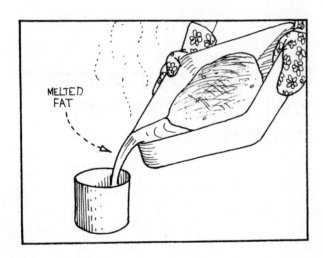

MELTED FAT

11

Take the dish out of the oven. It is **hot**. Use an oven mitt. Carefully pour off the fat into an old tin.

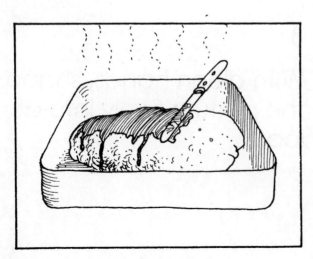

12

Spread the tomato sauce on top of the hot loaf.

13

Put the baking dish back into the oven. The dish is **hot**. Use an oven mitt.

OVEN-MITT

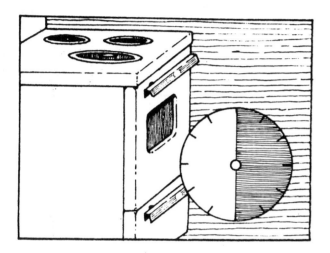

14

Bake the loaf for another 30 minutes.

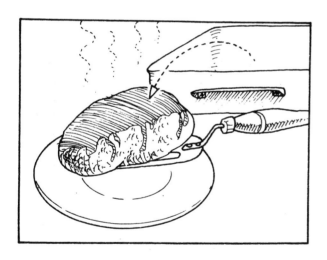

15

Carefully take the baking dish out of the oven. The dish is **hot.** Use an oven mitt. Put the loaf on to a plate. Turn the oven **off**.

16

Serve the loaf hot or cold. Slice the loaf with a knife.

Sausage Bake

For 4 people

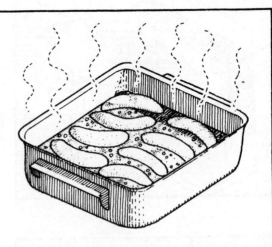

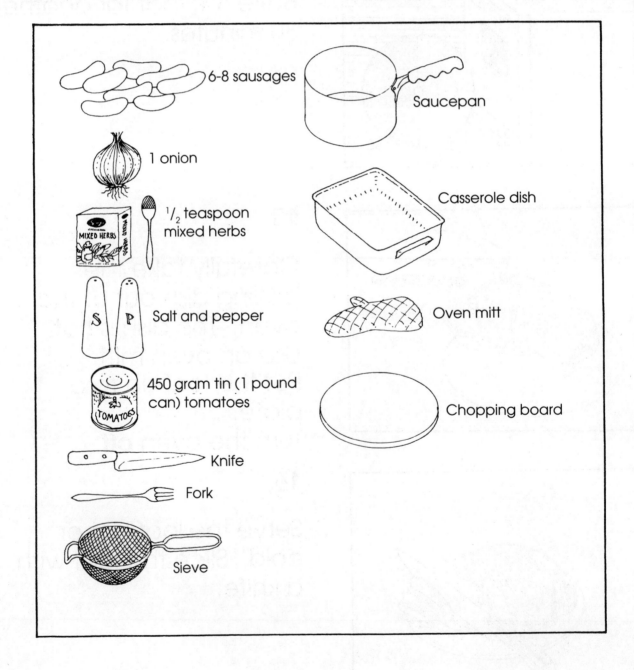

6-8 sausages

1 onion

1/2 teaspoon mixed herbs

Salt and pepper

450 gram tin (1 pound can) tomatoes

Knife

Fork

Sieve

Saucepan

Casserole dish

Oven mitt

Chopping board

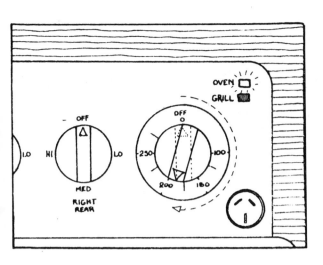

1 **Wash your hands.**

Turn the oven on to 180 deg. C (350 deg. F, gas mark 4).

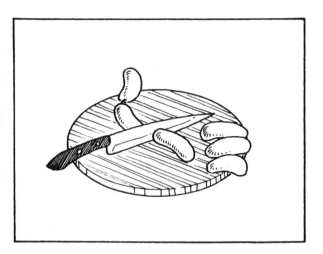

2

Separate the sausages with a knife.

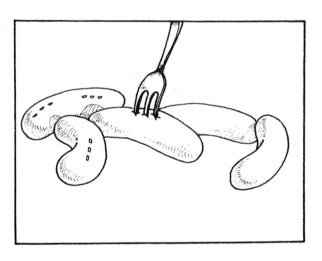

3

Prick each sausage with a fork.

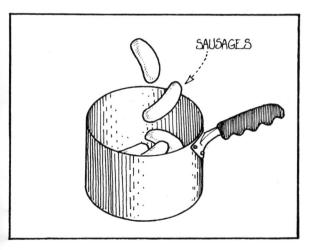

4

Put the sausages into the saucepan.

5

Cover the sausages with cold water.

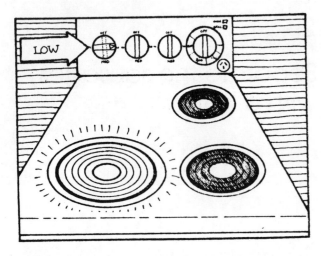

6

Turn the ring on to **low**.

7

Place the saucepan on to the ring so it can boil.

8

Simmer the sausages for 5 minutes.

136

9

Drain the sausages using the sieve.

10

Place the sausages into the casserole dish.

11

Chop up the onion finely.

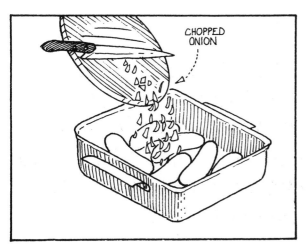

12

Sprinkle the onion over the sausages.

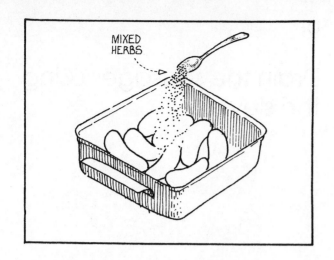

13

Sprinkle the mixed herbs over the sausages.

14

Sprinkle a pinch of salt and pepper over the sausages.

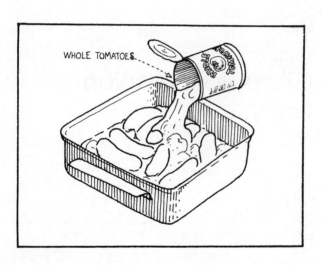

15

Pour the whole can of tomatoes over the sausages.

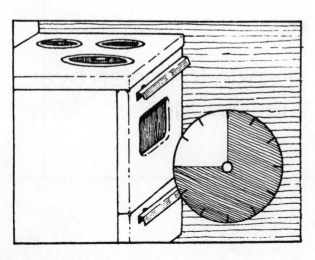

16

Place the casserole dish into the oven for 45 minutes. Then take it out. The dish is **hot**. Use an oven mitt. Turn the oven **off**.

Savoury Pie

For 4-6 people

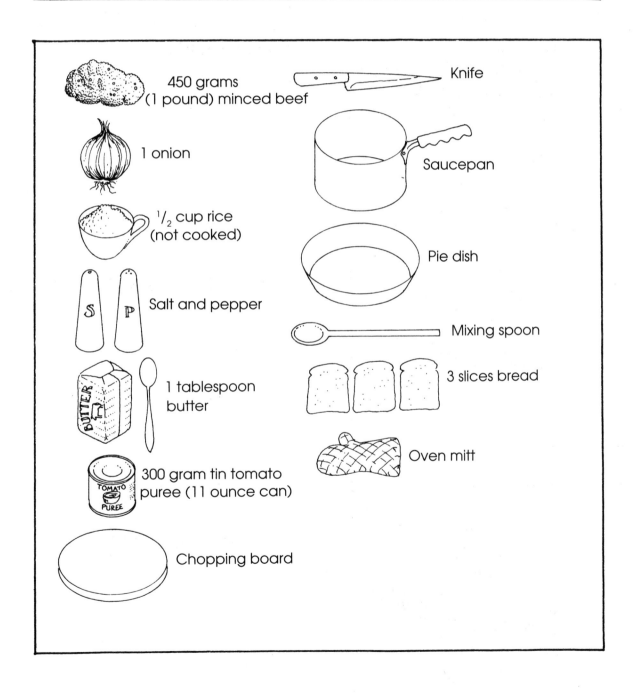

450 grams (1 pound) minced beef

Knife

1 onion

Saucepan

1/2 cup rice (not cooked)

Pie dish

Salt and pepper

Mixing spoon

1 tablespoon butter

3 slices bread

300 gram tin tomato puree (11 ounce can)

Oven mitt

Chopping board

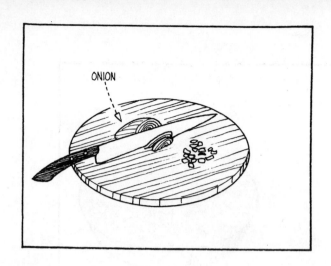

1 **Wash your hands.**

Chop up the onion finely.

2

Put the onion into the saucepan.

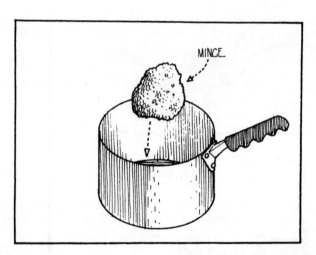

3

Add the minced beef.

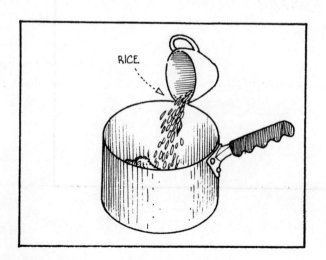

4

Add the uncooked rice.

5

Add a pinch of salt and pepper.

6

Add the tin of tomato puree.

7

Mix it all together really well.

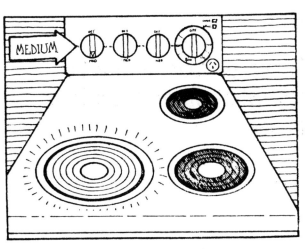

8

Turn the ring on to **medium**.

9

Place the saucepan on the ring so it can boil.

10

Stir the mixture all the time.

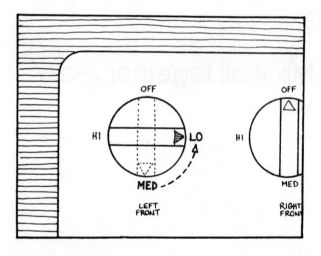

11

Turn the ring on to **low**.

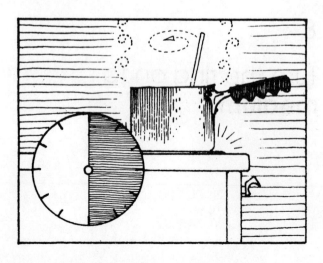

12

Simmer gently for 30 minutes stirring all the time.

142

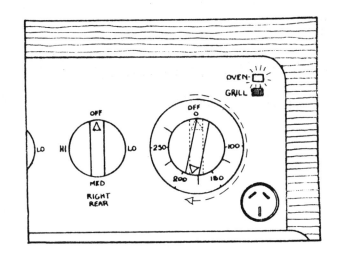

13

Turn the **oven** on to 180 deg. C (350 deg. F, gas mark 4).

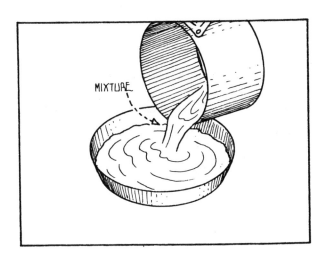

14

Pour the mixture evenly into the pie dish.

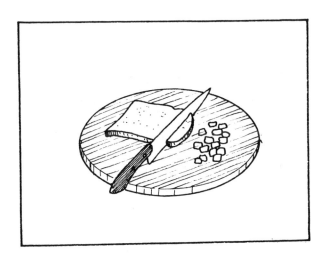

15

Cut the bread into tiny cubes.

16

Sprinkle the cubes over the mixture in the pie dish.

17

Put dots of butter on top of the mixture.

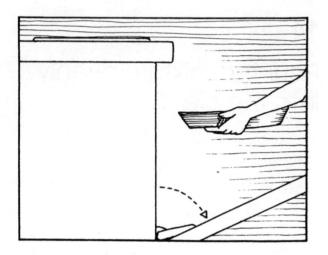

18

Open the oven door and place the pie dish into the oven. Bake for 15 minutes.

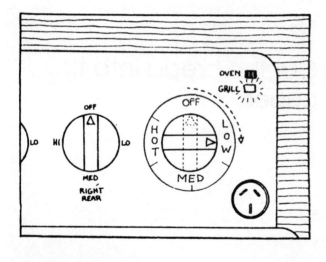

19

When 15 minutes is up turn the **oven off** and turn the **grill on** to low. WAIT till the top of the pie is golden brown.

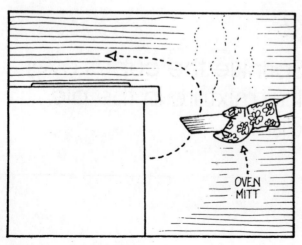

20

Open the grill door and place the baking dish on top of the stove.
The dish is **hot**. Use an oven mitt. Turn the grill **off**.

144

Dessert

Banana Pops

For 6 people

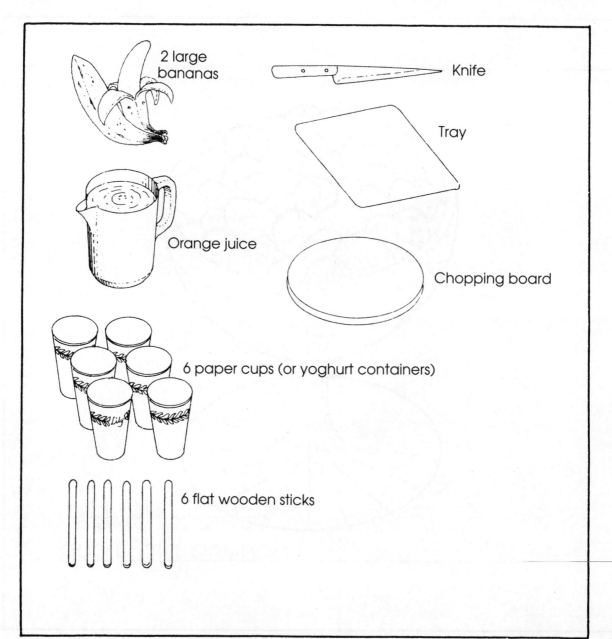

2 large bananas

Knife

Tray

Orange juice

Chopping board

6 paper cups (or yoghurt containers)

6 flat wooden sticks

146

1 **Wash your hands.**

Peel the bananas.

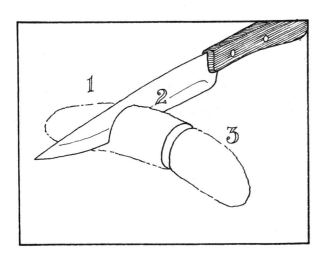

2

Cut each banana into 3 pieces.

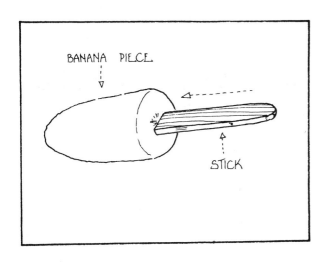

BANANA PIECE

STICK

3

Gently push a stick into each piece of banana.

4

Place each piece of banana into a cup.

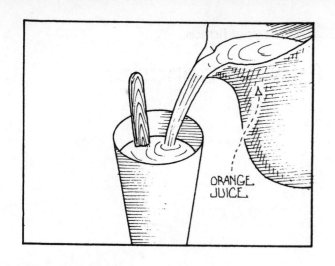

5

Pour in orange juice so that it covers the banana.

6

Divide the juice among the 6 cups.

7

Put the six cups into the freezer until set.

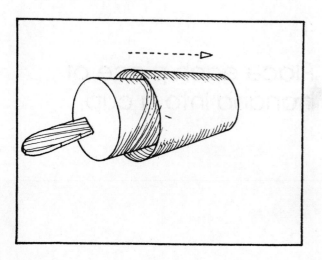

8

When set, remove the paper cups.

Fruit
Salad

For 3 people

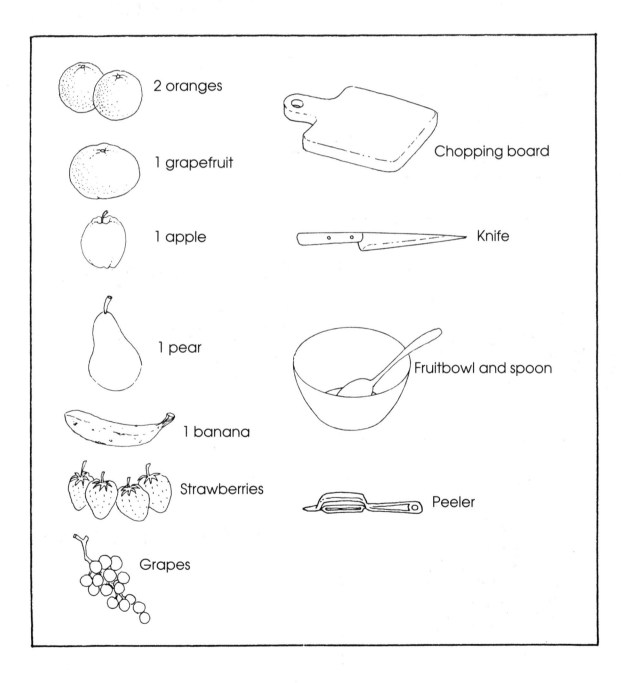

2 oranges

1 grapefruit

1 apple

1 pear

1 banana

Strawberries

Grapes

Chopping board

Knife

Fruitbowl and spoon

Peeler

1 **Wash your hands.**

Peel the oranges.

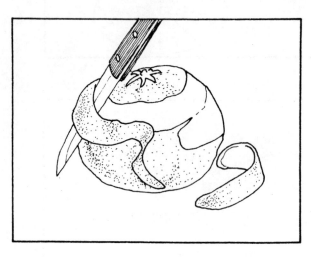

2

Peel the grapefruit.

3

Slice the oranges and grapefruit on the chopping board using the knife.

ORANGE AND GRAPEFRUIT PIECES

4

Put them in the bowl.

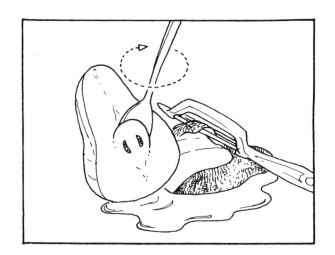

5

Peel and core the pear.

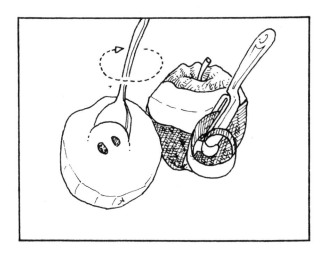

6

Peel and core the apple.

7

Cut the apple and pear into small cubes.

APPLE AND PEAR CUBES

8

Put them into the bowl. (The juice from the orange and grapefruit will stop them from turning brown.)

9

Wash the grapes.

10

Halve the grapes.

GRAPE HALVES

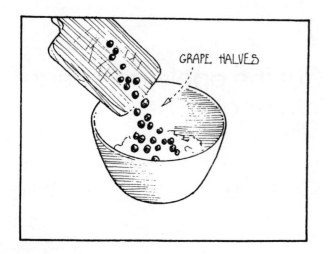

11

Put the grapes in the bowl.

GRAPE HALVES

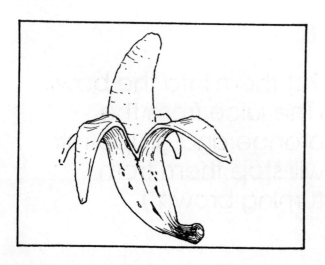

12

Peel the banana.

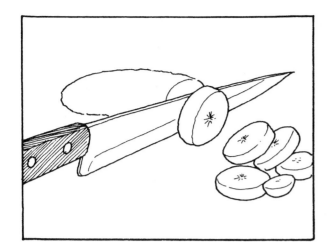

13

Slice the banana.

BANANA
SLICES

14

Add the banana to the bowl.

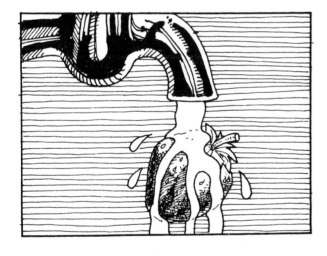

15

Wash the strawberries.

STRAWBERRY
HALVES

16

Halve the strawberries.

STRAWBERRY HALVES

17

Put the strawberries into the bowl.

18

Stir the fruits together with the spoon.

154

Creamy Pineapple

For 6 people

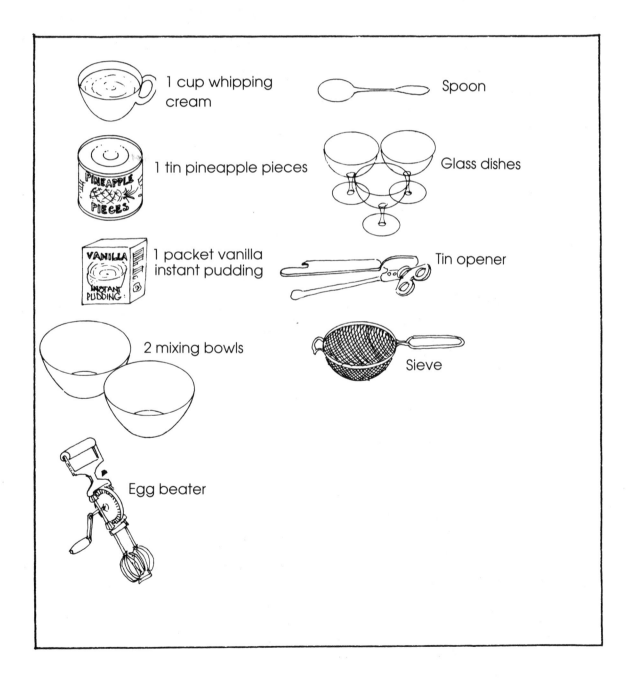

1 cup whipping cream

1 tin pineapple pieces

1 packet vanilla instant pudding

2 mixing bowls

Egg beater

Spoon

Glass dishes

Tin opener

Sieve

1 **Wash your hands.**

Put the whipping cream into one of the mixing bowls.

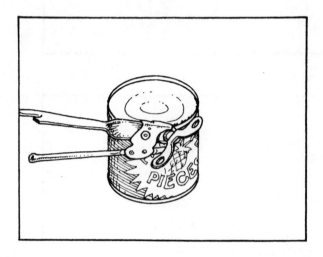

2

Carefully open the tin of pineapple with the tin opener.

3

Drain the tin of pineapple using the sieve.

4

Stir the pineapple juice into the cream.

156

5

Sprinkle 1 packet of vanilla instant pudding into the bowl of cream and juice.

6

Beat until it is thick using the egg beater.

7

Add the pineapple pieces and stir.

8

Spoon the pudding into 6 nice glass dishes. Put the dishes into the fridge for 30 minutes.

Apple Crunch

For 4-6 people

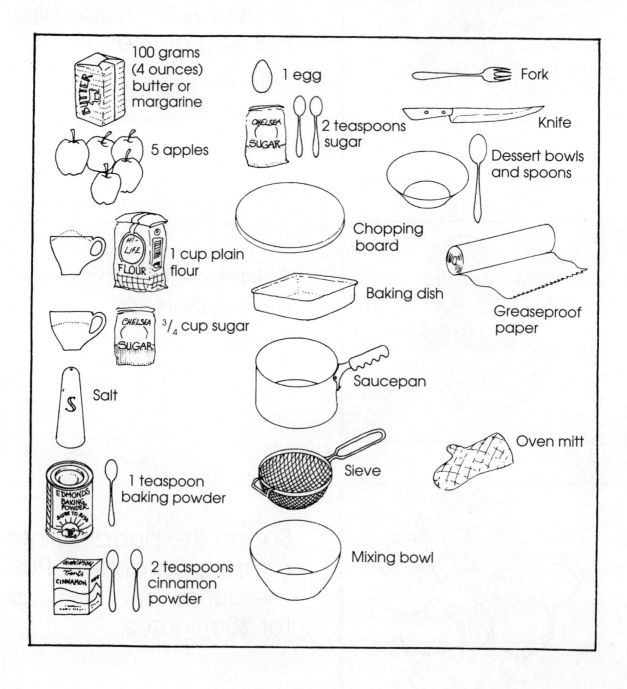

100 grams (4 ounces) butter or margarine

5 apples

1 cup plain flour

3/4 cup sugar

Salt

1 teaspoon baking powder

2 teaspoons cinnamon powder

1 egg

2 teaspoons sugar

Fork

Knife

Dessert bowls and spoons

Chopping board

Baking dish

Greaseproof paper

Saucepan

Sieve

Oven mitt

Mixing bowl

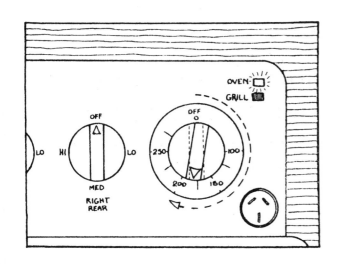

1 **Wash your hands.**

Turn the **oven** on to 180 deg C (350 deg F, gas mark 4).

2

Put a little bit of butter on to a piece of greaseproof paper. Spread the butter around the baking dish to lightly grease it.

3

Put the rest of the butter into the saucepan.

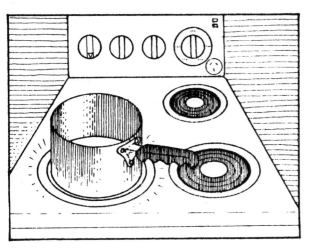

4

Turn the ring on to **low**.

Put the saucepan on the ring and gently melt the butter.

5

Take the saucepan of melted butter off the stove. Let it cool. Turn the ring **off**.

6

Peel and slice the apples.

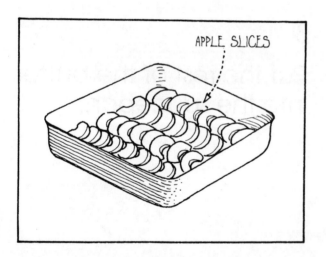

APPLE SLICES

7

Place the sliced apples in the baking dish.

FLOUR

8

Sift the cup of plain flour into the mixing bowl.

160

9

Sift the teaspoon of baking powder into the bowl.

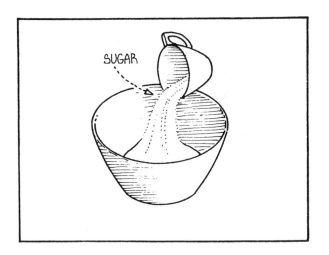

10

Add the sugar.

11

Add a pinch of salt.

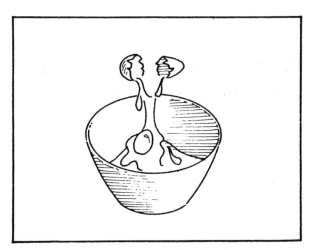

12

Break in one egg.

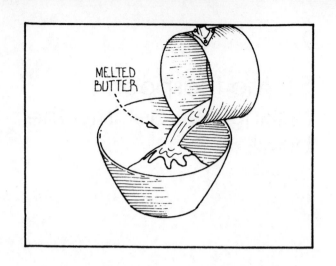

13

Pour in the melted butter.

14

Beat the mixture well with a fork.

15

Spread the mixture evenly over the apples in the baking dish.

16

Sprinkle the cinnamon over the mixture.

17

Sprinkle the sugar over the mixture.

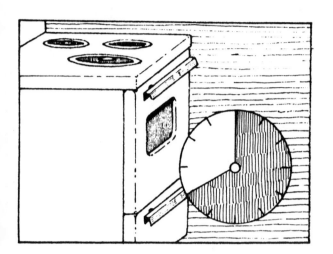

18

Put the baking dish into the oven. Bake for 40 minutes.

19

Take the dish out of the oven. It is **hot.** Use an oven mitt. Turn the oven **off**.

20

Dish the apple crunch into dessert bowls. Add cream or ice-cream.

Apple Sponge

For 4-6 people

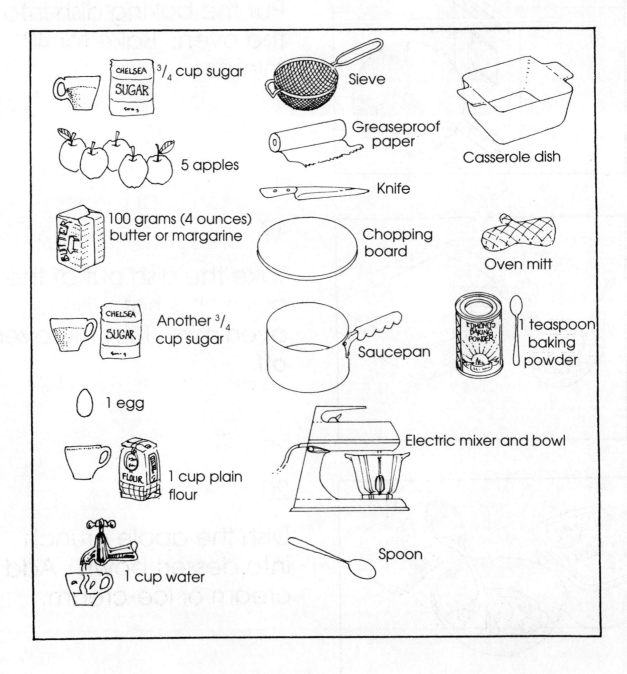

$^3/_4$ cup sugar

5 apples

100 grams (4 ounces) butter or margarine

Another $^3/_4$ cup sugar

1 egg

1 cup plain flour

1 cup water

Sieve

Greaseproof paper

Knife

Chopping board

Saucepan

Electric mixer and bowl

Spoon

Casserole dish

Oven mitt

1 teaspoon baking powder

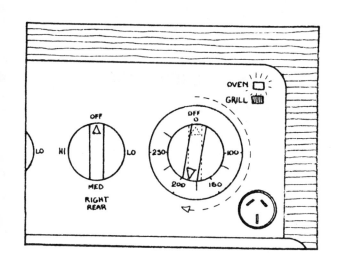

1 **Wash your hands.**

Turn the **oven** on to 180 deg. C (350 deg. F, gas mark 4).

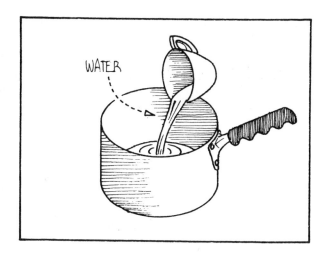

2

Put $^3/_4$ cup of water into the saucepan.

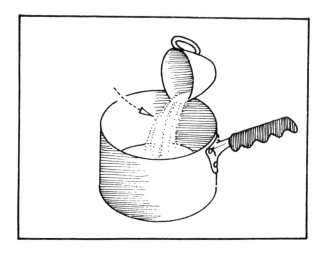

3

Add $^3/_4$ cup of sugar.

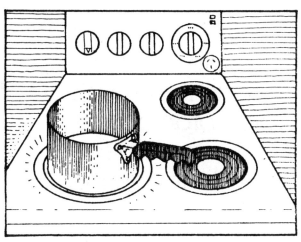

4

Turn the ring on to **medium**. Boil the sugar and water.

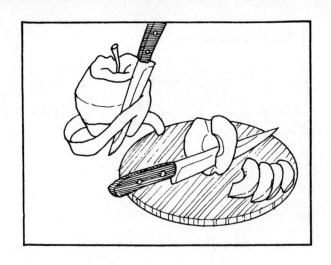

5

Peel and slice the apples.

6

Add the apples carefully to the boiling water.

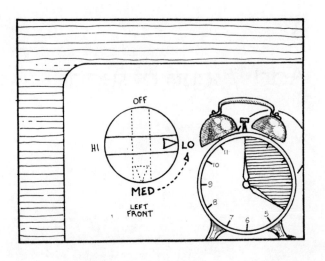

7

Turn the ring from medium to **low**. Simmer for 20 minutes till tender.

8

Put some butter or margarine on a piece of greaseproof paper. Grease the casserole dish with the paper.

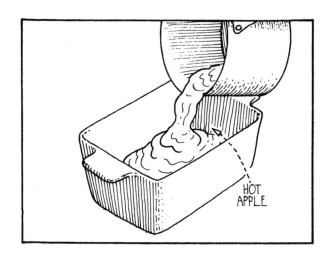

9

Pour the hot apples and juice into the casserole dish.

Turn the ring **off**.

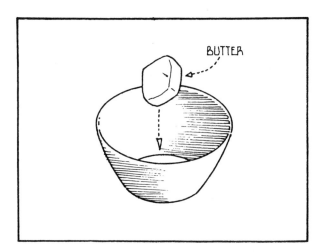

10

Put the rest of the butter or margarine into the mixing bowl.

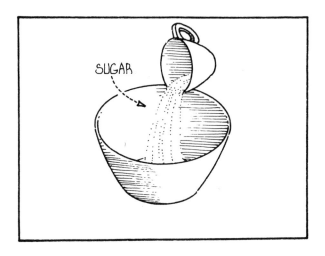

11

Add the other $^3/_4$ cup of sugar.

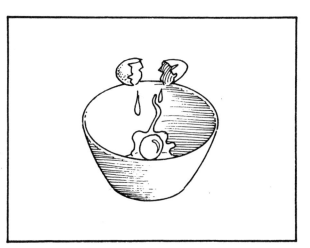

12

Break in 1 egg.

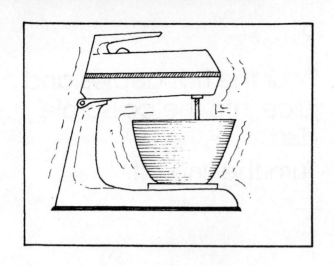

13

Beat the mixture with the electric mixer till creamy.

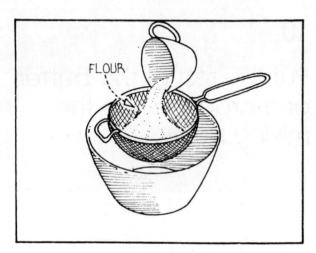

14

Sift in the plain flour.

15

Add the teaspoon of baking powder.

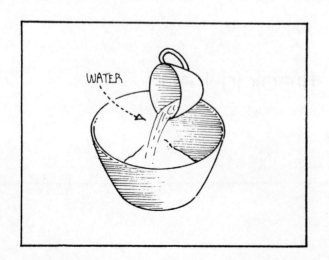

16

Add $\frac{1}{4}$ cup of water.

168

17

Beat the mixture well using the electric mixer.

18

Pour the mixture over the hot apples.

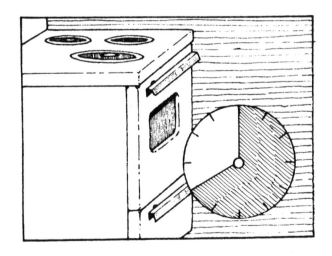

19

Put the casserole dish into the oven. Bake it for 40 minutes.
Then take it out of the oven.
The dish is **hot**. Use an oven mitt. Turn the oven **off**.

Hot Peaches

For 3 people

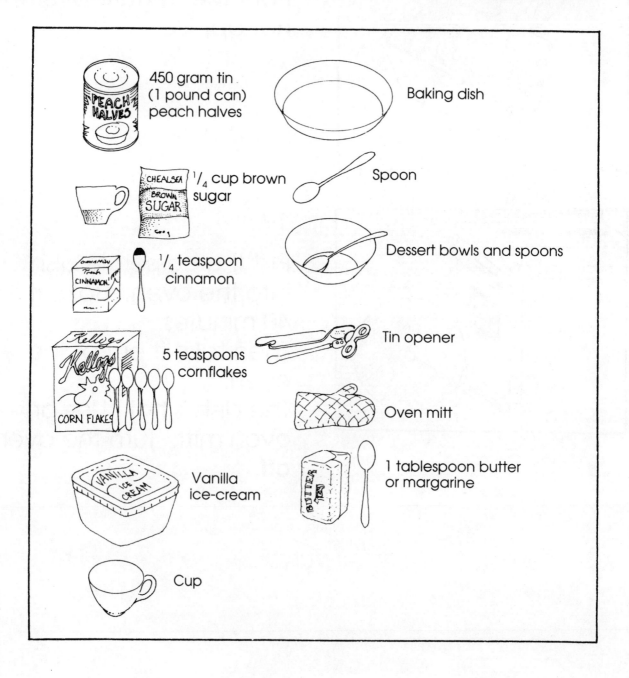

450 gram tin (1 pound can) peach halves

Baking dish

1/4 cup brown sugar

Spoon

1/4 teaspoon cinnamon

Dessert bowls and spoons

5 teaspoons cornflakes

Tin opener

Oven mitt

Vanilla ice-cream

1 tablespoon butter or margarine

Cup

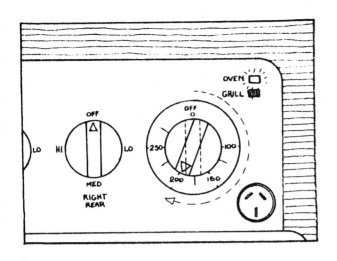

1 **Wash your hands.**

Turn the oven on to 190 deg. C (375 deg. F, gas mark 5)

2

Open the can of peaches.

3

Put the peach halves in a baking dish.

4

Gently pour the peach juice into the dish but **not** on top of the peach halves.

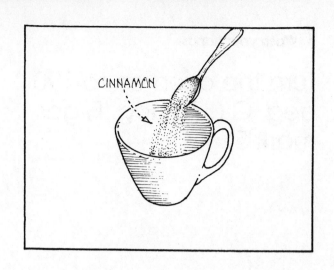

5

Put the cinnamon into a cup.

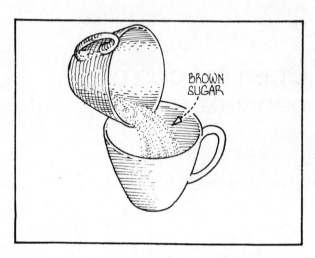

6

Add the brown sugar. Stir it together with the cinnamon.

7

Sprinkle the cinnamon and sugar mixture evenly over the peaches.

8

Sprinkle 1 teaspoon of cornflakes on each peach.

172

9

Place a small piece of butter on top of each peach.

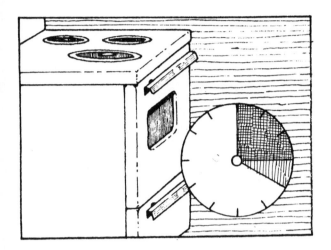

10

Open the oven door and put the baking dish inside. Bake for 15 to 20 minutes.

11

Take the dish out of the oven. The dish is **hot**. Use an oven mitt. Turn the oven **off**.

12

Place 1 peach half into each dessert bowl. Put a spoon of ice-cream on top of each peach.

Baking

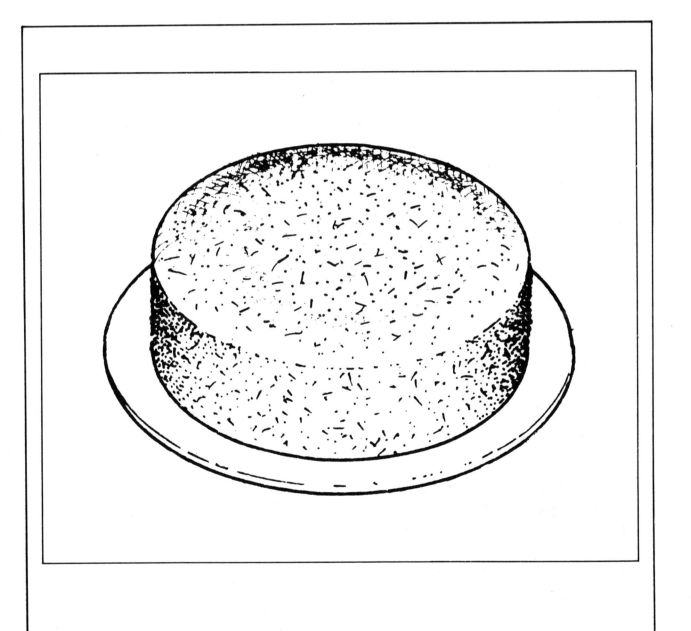

Banana Cake

For 6 people

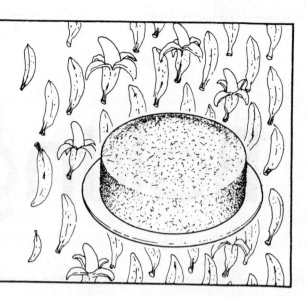

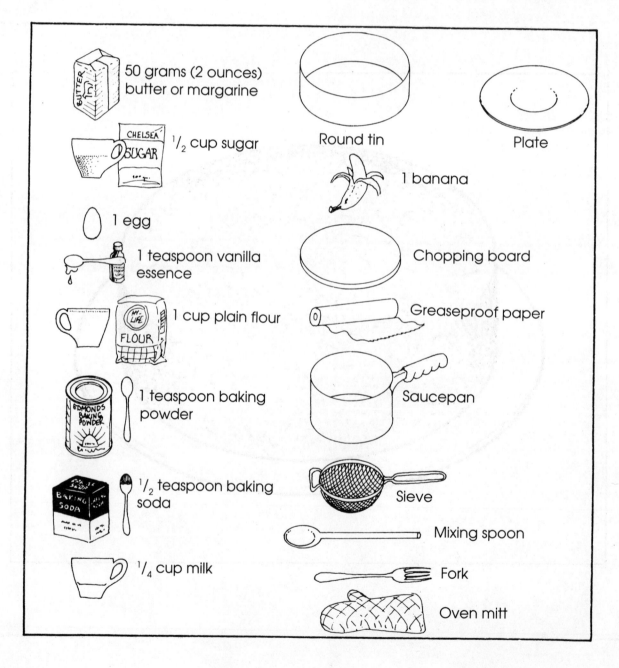

50 grams (2 ounces) butter or margarine

1/2 cup sugar

1 egg

1 teaspoon vanilla essence

1 cup plain flour

1 teaspoon baking powder

1/2 teaspoon baking soda

1/4 cup milk

Round tin

Plate

1 banana

Chopping board

Greaseproof paper

Saucepan

Sieve

Mixing spoon

Fork

Oven mitt

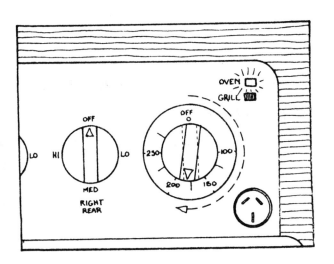

1 **Wash your hands.**

Turn the **oven** on to 180 deg. C (350 deg. C, gas mark 4).

2

Put some butter on to the paper. Grease the tin with butter using the greaseproof paper.

3

Sprinkle the tin lightly with flour.

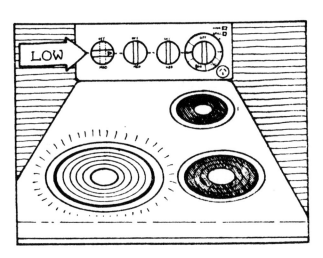

4

Turn the ring on to **low**.

5

Put the butter into the saucepan.

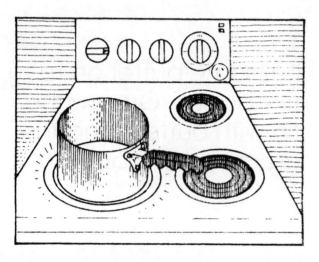

6

Put the saucepan on the ring and gently melt the butter.

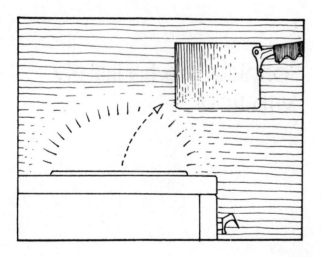

7

Take the saucepan off the stove. Turn the ring **off**.

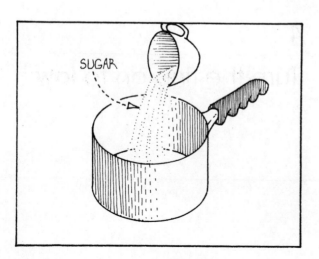

8

Add the sugar.

178

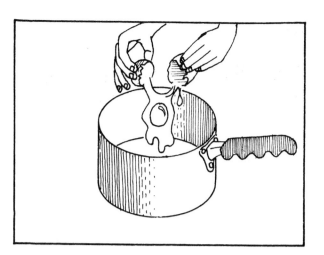

9

Break in 1 egg.

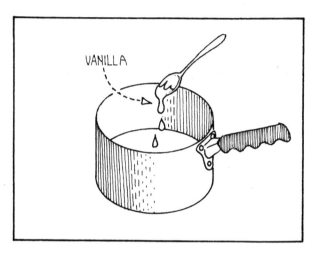

10

Add 1 teaspoon of vanilla essence.

11

Beat the mixture well with the wooden spoon until smooth.

12

Sift in the cup of plain flour.

13

Add the baking powder.

14

Add the baking soda.

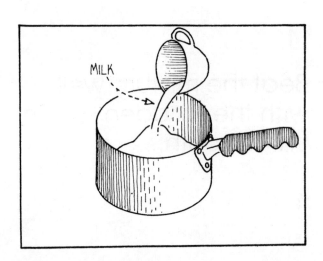

15

Add the milk.

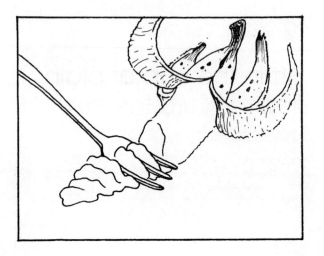

16

Peel the banana. Mash the banana with the fork on the chopping board.

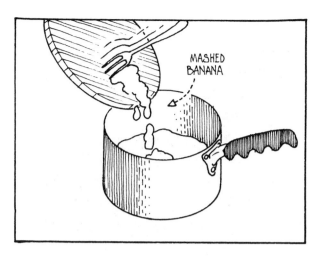

17
Add the mashed banana to the mixture and stir the mixture with a fork until just mixed.

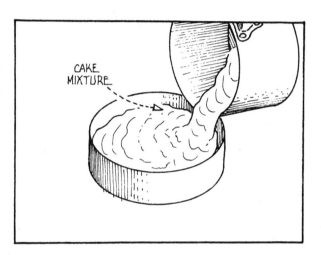

18
Pour all of the mixture into the tin.

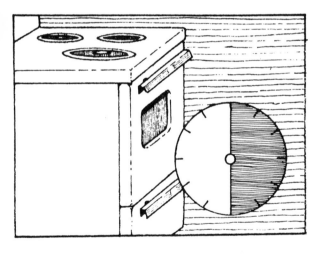

19
Put the tin into the oven. Bake the cake for 30 minutes. Take the cake out of the oven. The tin is **hot.** Use an oven mitt. Turn the oven **off**.

20
Wait for the cake to cool slightly. Turn the tin upside down over a plate and shake it gently to remove the cake.

Chocolate Cake

For 6 people

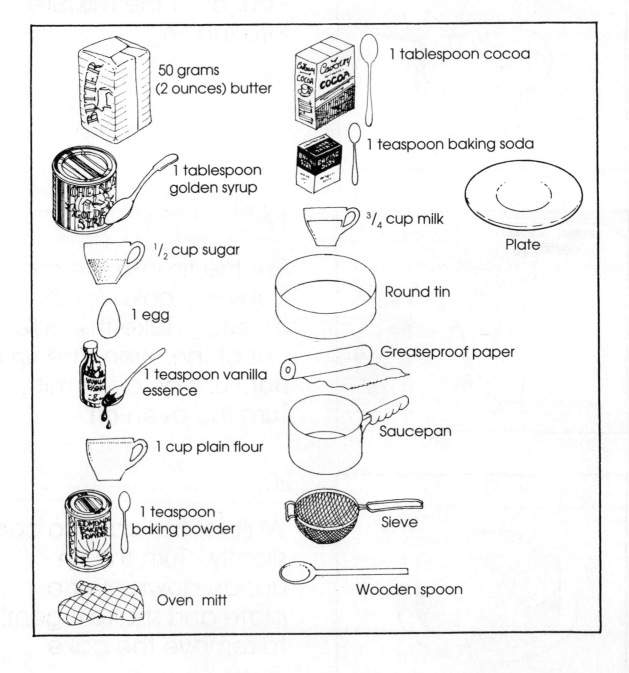

50 grams (2 ounces) butter

1 tablespoon golden syrup

1/2 cup sugar

1 egg

1 teaspoon vanilla essence

1 cup plain flour

1 teaspoon baking powder

Oven mitt

1 tablespoon cocoa

1 teaspoon baking soda

3/4 cup milk

Plate

Round tin

Greaseproof paper

Saucepan

Sieve

Wooden spoon

182

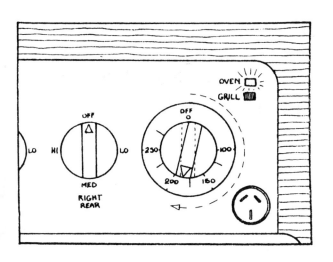

1 **Wash your hands.**

Turn the **oven** on to 180 deg. C (350 deg. F, gas mark 4).

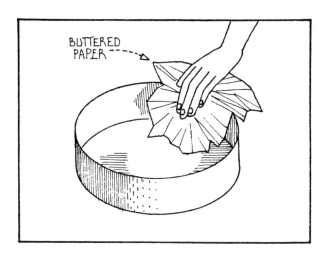

BUTTERED PAPER

2

Put some butter on the paper. Grease the tin with butter.

FLOUR

3

Sprinkle the tin lightly with flour.

BUTTER

4

Put the butter into the saucepan.

5

Add 1 tablespoon of golden syrup.

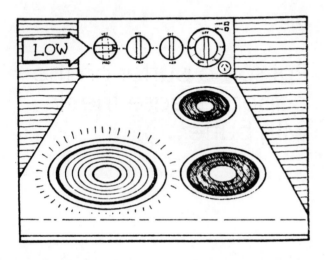

6

Turn the ring on to **low**.

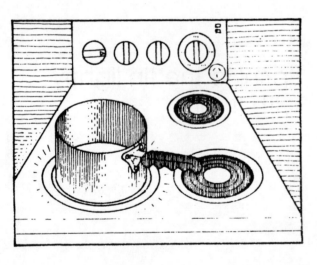

7

Put the saucepan on the ring and gently melt the butter and golden syrup. **Don't** let it boil.

8

Take the saucepan off the stove. Turn the ring **off**.

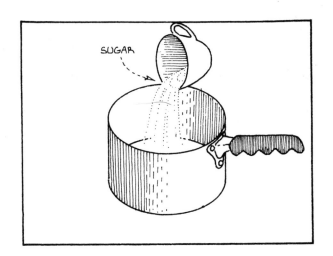

9

Add the sugar to the saucepan.

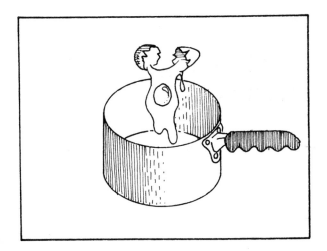

10

Break in 1 egg.

11

Add 1 teaspoon of vanilla essence.

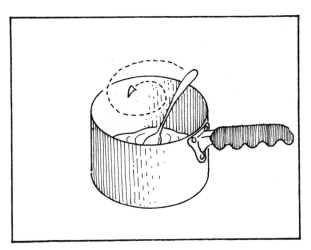

12

Stir the mixture well.

13

Sift in the cup of plain flour.

14

Add the teaspoon of baking powder.

15

Add the tablespoon of cocoa.

16

Fill a cup $^3/_4$ full of milk. Add the teaspoon of baking soda and stir.

17

Pour the cup of milk and baking soda into the mixture in the saucepan. Stir and mix well.

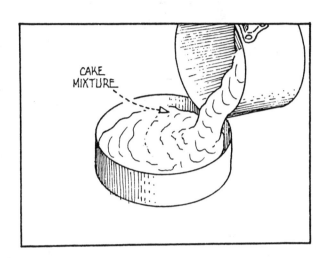

18

Pour all of the mixture into the tin.

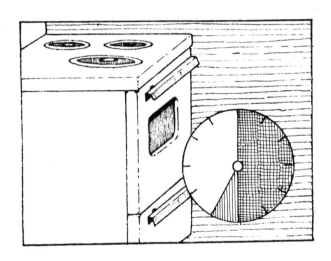

19

Put the tin into the oven. Bake the cake for 30-35 minutes. Take the cake out of the oven. The tin is **hot**. Use an oven mitt. Turn the oven **off**.

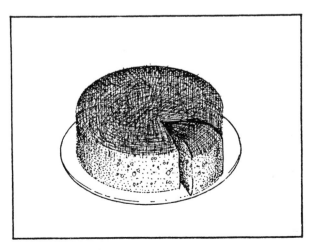

20

Wait for the cake to cool slightly. Turn the tin upside down on to a plate and shake gently to remove the cake.

Rum Balls

For 4-6 people

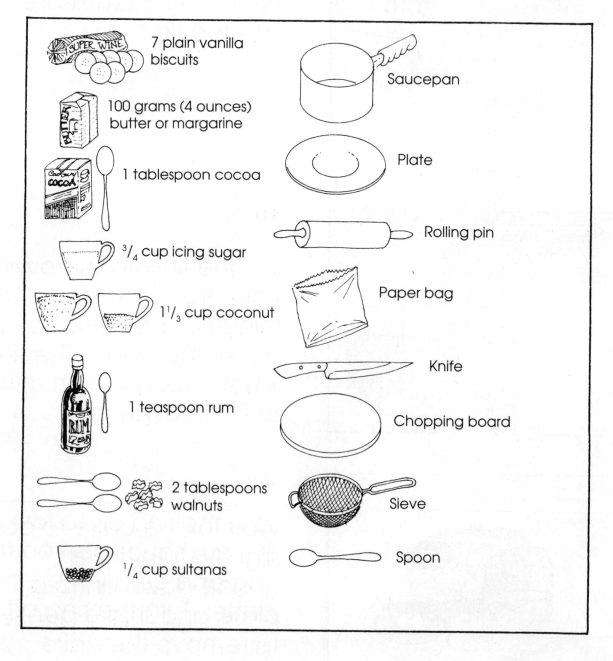

7 plain vanilla biscuits

100 grams (4 ounces) butter or margarine

1 tablespoon cocoa

$^3/_4$ cup icing sugar

$1^1/_3$ cup coconut

1 teaspoon rum

2 tablespoons walnuts

$^1/_4$ cup sultanas

Saucepan

Plate

Rolling pin

Paper bag

Knife

Chopping board

Sieve

Spoon

1 **Wash your hands.**

Put some biscuits into the paper bag.

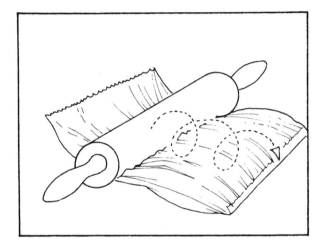

2

Roll the paper bag with the rolling pin till the biscuits are finely crushed.

3

Put the butter into the saucepan.

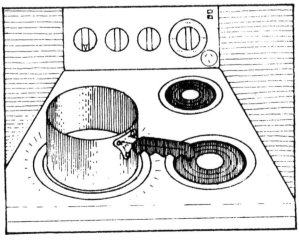

4

Turn the ring on to **low**. Put the saucepan on the ring and gently melt the butter. Turn the ring **off**.

5

Sift the cocoa into the melted butter.

6

Add the icing sugar.

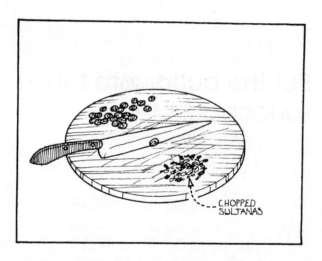

7

Chop up the sultanas until they are very small using the chopping board and knife.

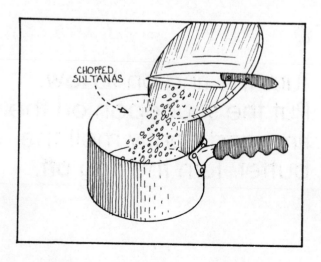

8

Add the sultanas to the saucepan.

190

9

Add 1 teaspoon of rum.

10

Add $\frac{1}{3}$ cup of coconut.

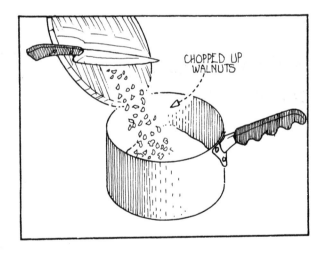

11

Chop up the walnuts till they are very small. Put the walnuts into the saucepan.

12

Add the biscuit crumbs to the saucepan.

13

Stir the mixture well.

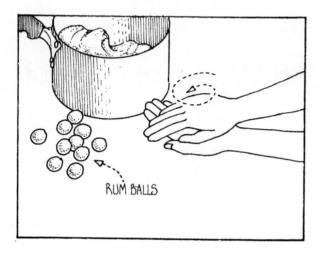

RUM BALLS

14

Roll the mixture into small balls.

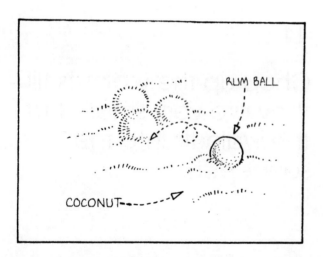

RUM BALL

COCONUT

15

Roll the balls lightly in the coconut.

16

Roll the balls on to a plate.

192

Butter Cookies

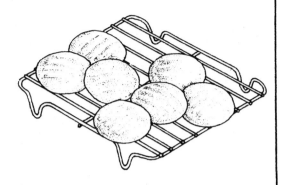

For 4-6 people

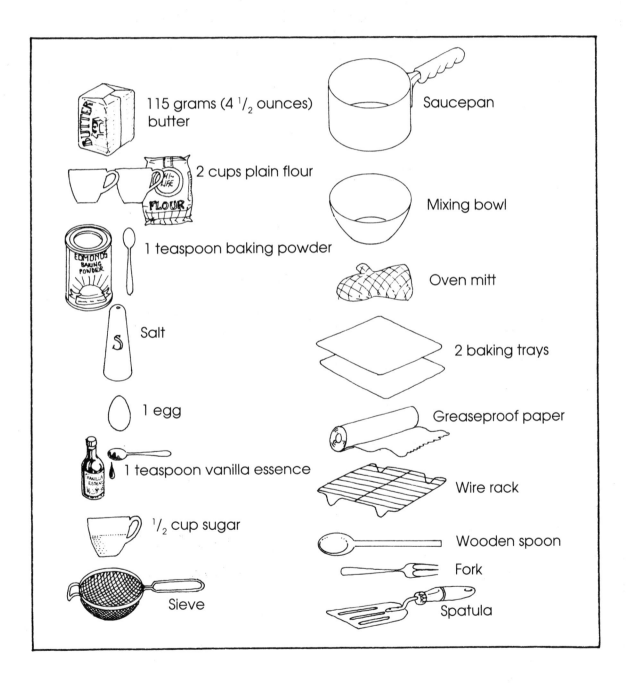

115 grams (4 ½ ounces) butter

2 cups plain flour

1 teaspoon baking powder

Salt

1 egg

1 teaspoon vanilla essence

½ cup sugar

Sieve

Saucepan

Mixing bowl

Oven mitt

2 baking trays

Greaseproof paper

Wire rack

Wooden spoon

Fork

Spatula

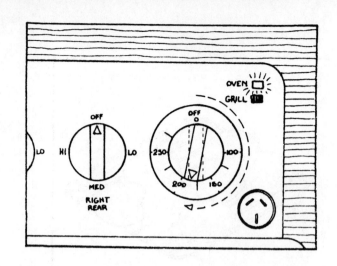

1 Wash your hands.

Turn the oven on to 180 deg. C (350 deg. F, gas mark 4).

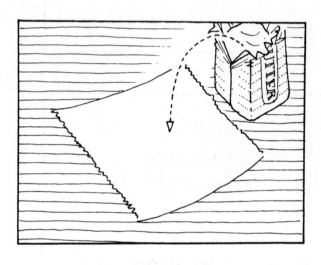

2

Put some butter on to the paper.

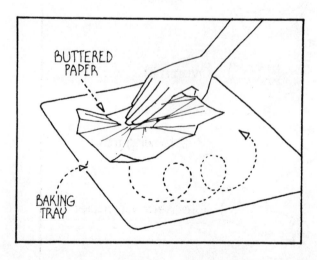

3

Rub the butter on to the baking trays to lightly grease them.

4

Sprinkle a little bit of flour over the tray.

194

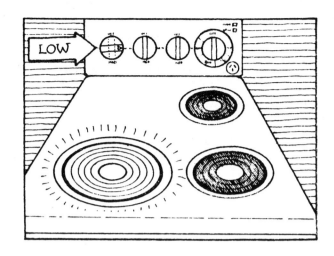

5

Turn the ring on to **low**.

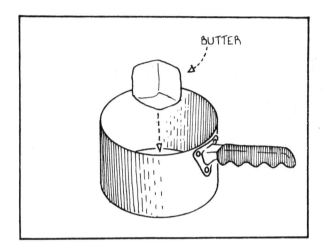

6

Put the butter into the saucepan.

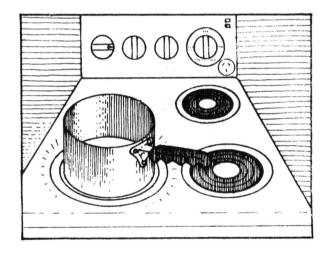

7

Put the saucepan on to the ring and gently melt the butter.

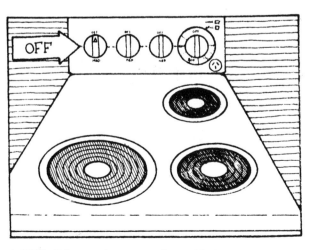

8

When the butter has melted, take the saucepan off the stove. Turn the ring **off**.

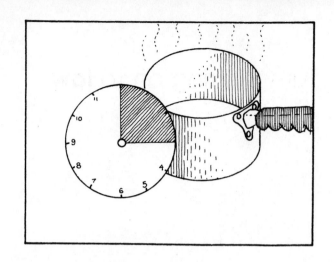

9

Cool the butter for 15 minutes.

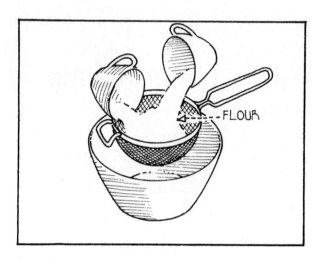

10

Meanwhile, sift the plain flour into the bowl.

11

Sift the baking powder into the bowl.

12

Sprinkle a pinch of salt into the bowl.

13

Break 1 egg into the saucepan with the melted butter.

14

Put 1 teaspoon of vanilla essence into the saucepan.

15

Put the sugar into the saucepan.

16

Beat the mixture well with the wooden spoon.

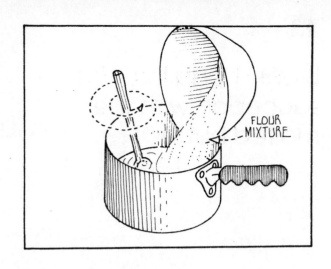

17

Stir in the sifted flour mixture (from the bowl) into the saucepan.

18

Stir everything in the saucepan all together.

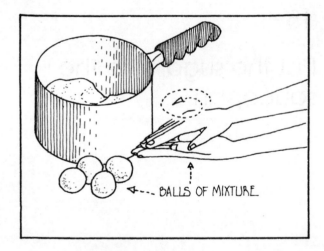

19

Put small lumps of the mixture into you hand and roll into balls.

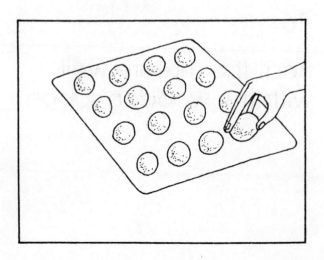

20

Place the balls on to the baking trays.

198

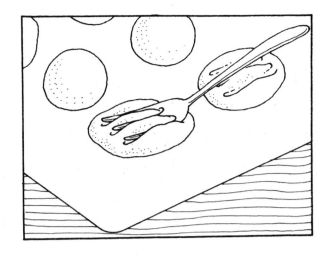

21

Flatten the balls lightly
with a fork.

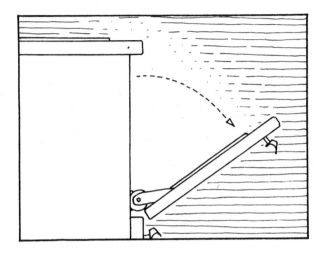

22

Open the oven door.

23

Put the trays into the
oven.

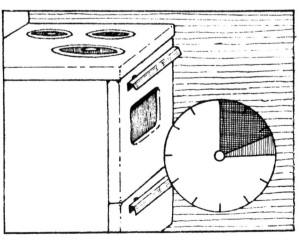

24

Wait 12-15 minutes for
the cookies to cook in
the oven.

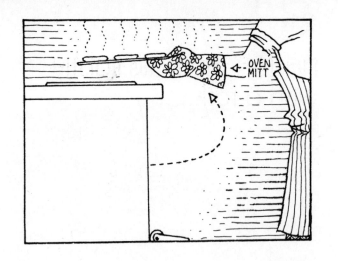

25

Open the oven door and place the trays on top of the stove. The trays are **hot.** Use an oven mitt.

26

Use the spatula to place the cookies on to the wire rack to cool. Turn the oven **off**.

Coconut Cookies

For 4-6 people

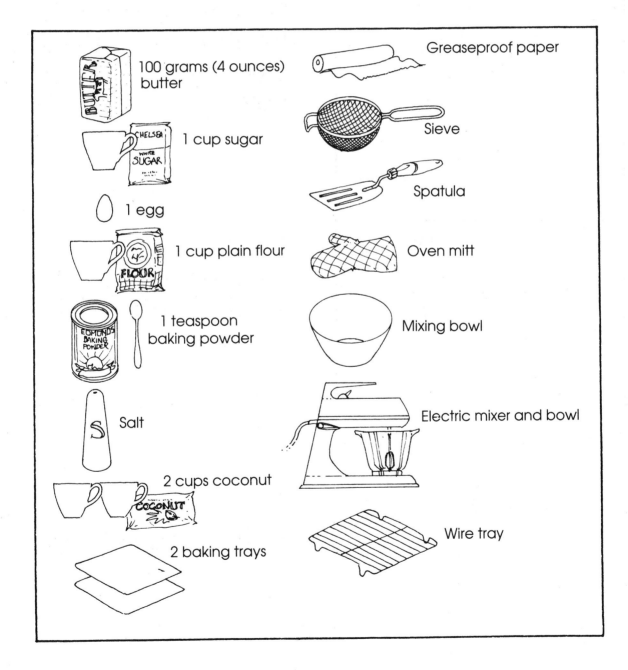

100 grams (4 ounces) butter

1 cup sugar

1 egg

1 cup plain flour

1 teaspoon baking powder

Salt

2 cups coconut

2 baking trays

Greaseproof paper

Sieve

Spatula

Oven mitt

Mixing bowl

Electric mixer and bowl

Wire tray

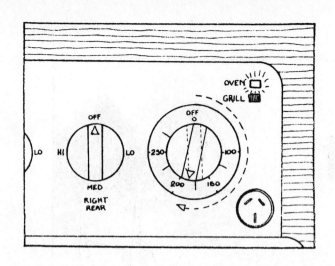

1 **Wash your hands.**

Turn the **oven** on to 180 deg. C (350 deg. F, gas mark 4).

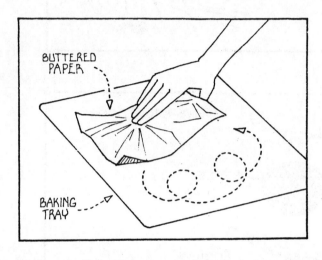

2

Put some butter on to the paper and use it to grease the 2 baking trays.

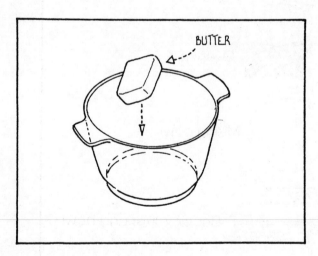

3

Put the butter into the electric mixer bowl.

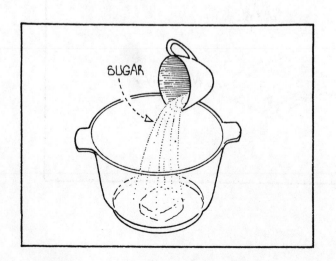

4

Add the cup of sugar.

5

Break in 1 egg.

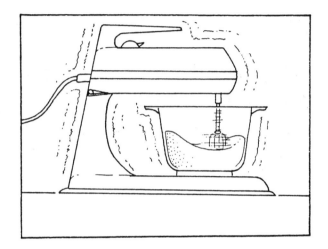

6

Beat the ingredients till well mixed.

7

Sift the cup of flour into a new bowl.

8

Sift the teaspoon of baking powder into the bowl.

9

Add a pinch of salt.

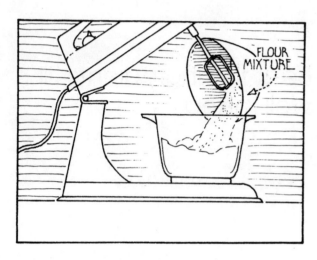

10

Add the flour mixture to the butter mixture. Mix well with the electric mixer.

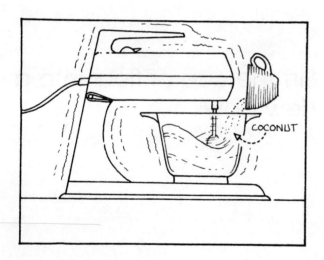

11

Slowly mix in the coconut - it will be very stiff.

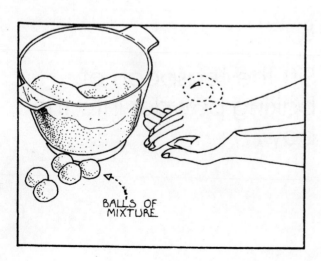

12

Roll the mixture into balls with your hands.

204

13

Place the balls on the 2 trays.

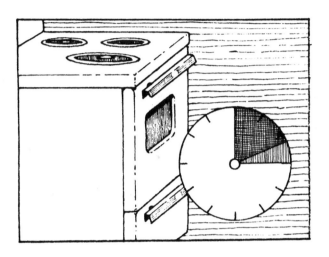

14

Place the trays inside the oven. Bake for 12 to 15 minutes.

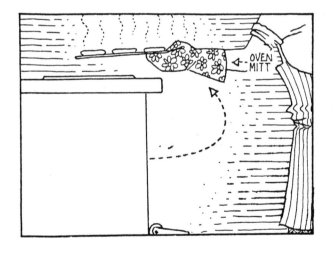

15

Open the oven door and place the trays on top of the stove. The trays are **hot**. Use an oven mitt. Turn the oven **off**.

16

Using the spatula, place the cookies on to a wire rack to cool.

206

Index